THE

POCKET

GURU

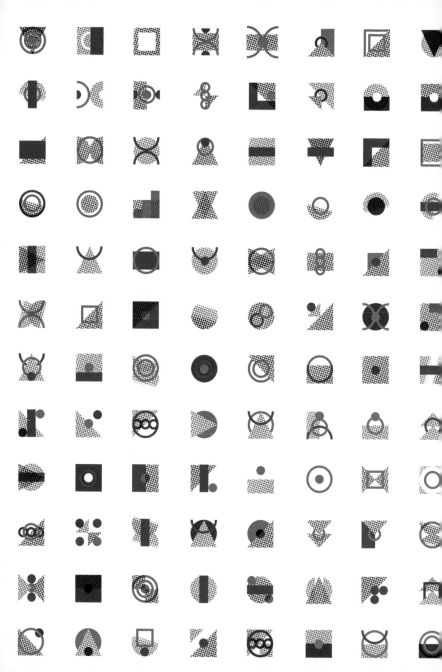

THE

POCKET

GURU

guidance and mantras for
SPIRITUAL AWAKENING
and
EMOTIONAL WISDOM

DR. SIRI SAT NAM

CHRONICLE BOOKS
SAN FRANCISCO

Library of Congress Cataloging-in-Publication Data:

Names: Nam, Siri Sat, author.

Title: The pocket guru / Siri Sat Nam, PhD, LMFT.

Description: San Francisco : Chronicle Books, [2019]

Identifiers: LCCN 2018027175 | ISBN 9781452174150 (hardcover : alk. paper)

Subjects: LCSH: Self. | Self-actualization (Psychology) | Meditation.

Classification: LCC BF697 .N36 2019 | DDC 158.1--dc23 LC record available at https://lccn.loc.gov/2018027175

Manufactured in China

FSC
www.fsc.org
MIX
Paper from
responsible sources
FSC® C008047

Design by Hillary Caudle

10 9 8 7 6 5 4 3 2 1

Chronicle books and gifts are available at special quantity discounts to corporations, professional associations, literacy programs, and other organizations. For details and discount information, please contact our corporate/premiums department at corporatesales@chroniclebooks.com or at 1-800-759-0190.

Chronicle Books LLC
680 Second Street
San Francisco, California 94107
www.chroniclebooks.com

Dedication

I WOULD LIKE TO DEDICATE THIS BOOK to my mother, stepfather, and those individuals on the maternal side (my aunt, grandmother, grandfather, and great-grandmother) who raised me with love and taught me respect of self and others. I thank you.

TABLE OF
CONTENTS

Introduction

IN MODERN DAY UNDERSTANDING, we usually think of a "guru" as a perfect being, a holy man or woman who is an incarnation of the Divine—a Mahan Rishi. The reality is that a guru is the intermediary between the individual and a higher power. Of course, guru consciousness can be embodied within a person, but, in this particular situation, the Spark of the Divine, the Light from Beyond, the Loving Guidance, will be lodged within a book. The function of any avatar, prophet, teacher, or guru is to transform darkness of mind into light. Indeed, this Pocket Guru is no different. It is a vehicle to deepen into wisdom. We all have the capacity to receive wisdom, if we but consciously sit, meditate, and wait to receive it.

The structure of *The Pocket Guru* is rooted in numerology, as it is comprised of 108 chapters—a number that is sacred in yogic tradition. The number 90 correlates to completion, perfection, fulfillment, and mastery, while 108 confirms that mastery has transpired.

Each chapter has 11 power statements to guide you in the mastery of that particular chapter's topic. First, skim the list of 108 chapter verses in the Table of Contents. Which one calls you? After you make a conscious choice of the topic, read through that chapter's power statements a few times. If you wish to begin gaining the blessings of those statements, commit to reciting them 11 times in one sitting as you deepen into manifestation. If you wish to change a habit, repeat this exercise for 40 days, a time span that has spiritual, historical significance. If you wish to perfect any of the 108 chapter verses, do the recitation for 90 days. To confirm your mastery, do it for 108 days.

While you are reciting the 11 power statements aloud from a chapter verse, consciously feel the words you are speaking. To manifest the blessing of the power statement, visualize the words inscribed on your forehead or listen deeply to what you are saying to merge with the meaning on an auditory level. Decide which mode, visual or auditory, is more primary for you.

The Pocket Guru also contains 11 meditation practices—eleven being the number that represents the guru (consciousness beyond the limitation of the individual mind). Each meditation will work on different aspects of your being (e.g., your intuition, your heart center). The Siddha (what can be achieved if the meditation is mastered, such as development of heightened intuition, expanded ability for compassion, and so on) introduces each meditation. Use these meditations to rid the subconscious mind of repressed psychic material and activate your personal growth.

Allow *The Pocket Guru* to propel your spiritual awareness, enhance mental calm, increase emotional intelligence, and cement success in your relationship to yourself and others. The experience will be yours. If you do the work, the work will, eventually, begin to work for you.

Addiction

ADDICTION IS THE SYNDROME in which someone is obsessed with something outside themselves to make them feel good. That something could be innumerable things such as drugs, food, sex, work, and even relationships. Those who are addicted compulsively act until they become possessed by the behaviors.

In giving up an addiction to one particular substance or activity, it is necessary to be cautious and not compulsively act out in another arena. For example, in giving up drugs, an individual can become addicted to cigarettes or food. Resolving addiction takes concentrated work. To overcome addictive behaviors, professional assistance is often needed to regain mental, physical, and emotional stability. But also allow the following 11 statements to inform and assist in the journey of overcoming addictive behaviors.

POWER STATEMENTS

1.   ADDICTION is obsession and compulsion.

2.   ADDICTION says that I need something outside of myself to make me feel good.

3. ADDICTION is a time-consuming, dysfunctional relationship with something outside myself.

4. ADDICTION offers a temporary moment of perceived pleasure and release from pain.

5. ADDICTION has disconnected me from what can be fun outside of my addictive behavior.

6. ADDICTION says I have uncomfortable feelings that I need to work through.

7. ADDICTION dissipates when I process abuse—physical, sexual, and neglect—that I have experienced.

8. ADDICTION points to internalized shame and the need to realign with unconditional self-love.

9. ADDICTION informs me that I must become aware that I am enough.

10. ADDICTION suggests I acknowledge my triggers and make different choices.

11. ADDICTION tells me it is okay to ask for help.

Alone

WITHIN OUR CULTURE we have not cultivated the art and science of being alone. Yes, it is comforting to have pleasant company, but can we also have an enjoyable time when we are simply alone?

The concept that we are whole within ourselves appears to have escaped the cultural narrative. Of course, other people can have attributes and qualities that give us a sense of fulfillment. But to think of ourselves as incomplete and in need of the company of others to be fulfilled is a premise that debilitates and sours the psyche.

To become aware that we are whole and complete within ourselves is an exhilarating thought. When we begin to think about ourselves as the delectable main course, then we can nurture ourselves. Meditation is one of the tools to enhance this sense of oneness.

POWER STATEMENTS

1. Being ALONE can activate the
    wish to be with someone.

2. Being ALONE is sometimes scary.

3. Being ALONE can arouse
    negative thoughts.

4. Being ALONE gives me time
    to hear my thoughts.

5. Being ALONE requires that I focus
    my thoughts on goodwill.

6. Being ALONE can be a respite
    from the busyness of life.

7. Being ALONE signals that it
    is time for meditation.

8. Being ALONE causes me to
    deepen into stillness.

9. Being ALONE is time to be
    with my individual soul.

10. Being ALONE is time to deepen into
    my oneness with the Divine.

11. Being ALONE evokes peace.

Anger

WITHIN OUR CULTURE we are commonly taught that we should suppress anger. Assuredly, anger has gotten a bad rap when it is expressed through physical assaults, domestic violence, war, road rage, murder, and horrid episodes of revenge—all of which are dysfunctional expressions of anger. Nonetheless, suppressing our anger is not the goal. Instead, we should seek to master the expression of our anger.

When another has insulted us, violated our boundaries, or disrespected our rights, and we consciously decide not to respectfully and peacefully express our anger, then we are delivering the message to the other that they can continue to inflict pain, discomfort, and disrespect.

Allow Dr. Martin Luther King Jr. to be an example of one who practiced this principle. It was he who was so angry and disgusted with segregation and the violation of black people's civil liberties that he organized a nation of people to protest in a manner that elevated the consciousness of the entire United States. To deny our anger is to silently reinforce insult to our person, violation of boundaries, and disrespect to self. But to channel our anger "effectively" has the possibility of creating positive change in the world at large.

POWER STATEMENTS

1. ANGER is an unsettling feeling.

2. ANGER stems from my unexpressed hurt.

3. ANGER is telling me to respect my hurt.

4. ANGER held in can hurt and negatively impact my health (e.g., heart problems, skin eruptions, etc.).

5. ANGER signals that I must effectively communicate.

6. ANGER effectively expressed will ignite my growth.

7. ANGER effectively expressed will ignite the other's growth.

8. ANGER is the fire inside me to create transformation.

9. ANGER effectively expressed can lead to positive change.

10. ANGER must be acknowledged.

11. ANGER acknowledged and effectively expressed says I am emotionally intelligent.

Anxiety

ANXIETY, WITH ITS UNSETTLING SYMPTOMS, such as insomnia, heart palpitations, sweaty palms or feet, is no fun. This disorder can incapacitate an individual and prevent daily functioning. The cause? The treatment? There is no one cause and no one treatment. But concentrating on the origin of one's anxiety and the triggers is the key to diminishing its impact. Reflection, deep breathing, and trying new ways of being in the world, along with a dedicated, daily meditative practice, can help bring relief.

POWER STATEMENTS

1. ANXIETY drains my mental
    and emotional energy.

2. ANXIETY is the nervousness that arises
    when I feel as if I have no control.

3. ANXIETY says I am obsessing
    on certain thoughts.

4. ANXIETY provokes me to process deep-
    seated, repressed psychic material.

5. ANXIETY subsides as I do free-flow writing.

6. ANXIETY is surmounted as I employ
    patience.

7. ANXIETY lessens as I embrace adventure
    and do something different.

8. ANXIETY alerts me to engage in life
    rather than worry about life.

9. ANXIETY wants to debilitate me, but I will
    divert it into efforts to achieve my goals.

10. ANXIETY recedes as I remember that life
    is constantly unfolding on my behalf.

11. ANXIETY dissipates as I meditate on
    the Divine and feel its protection.

Betrayal

BETRAYAL HURTS, it sears, it traumatizes. It destroys trust. What do we do after we have been deceived, dishonored, or devalued? The survivor, first of all, must acknowledge the collection of feelings (e.g., sadness, hurt, fear, anger) that have resulted as they face the reconstruction of the psyche. Understandably, we would rather run away from these uncomfortable feelings; yet, when we learn to sit in this darkness, a transformation into the Expanded Self becomes possible.

Everyone is not here to love us. Be clear about that. Within the universe there are snakes and sharks as well as doves and peacocks. We must use discernment as we attempt to live life.

POWER STATEMENTS

1. BETRAYAL hurts.

2. BETRAYAL hurts, but I'm still breathing.

3. BETRAYAL feels as if my heart has been extracted from my chest.

4. BETRAYAL asks me to acknowledge a violation of my boundaries, my trust, and/or my kindness.

5. BETRAYAL evokes despair.

6. BETRAYAL evokes anger.

7. BETRAYAL gives me an opportunity to go beyond my anger and feel my hurt.

8. BETRAYAL can be discussed to discern whether the other made an unconscious mistake.

9. BETRAYAL takes me out of idealism and into realism.

10. BETRAYAL can be avoided when I trust my intuition.

11. BETRAYAL hurts, and it takes time for my wounds to heal.

Body

THE BODY IS A GIFT FROM THE DIVINE. Respect and take care of it because, if we don't, the next eye will be glass, the next leg, prosthetic, and the next heart, a transplant. Be mindful: Each of us will get only one body in this lifetime. We should worship it as we feed, rest, and energize it. The body is our personal vehicle while on the planet. It transports us from one place to another. It is a gift from the Divine. It is the carrier of our living souls.

POWER STATEMENTS

1. My BODY is the vehicle that gets me around while on the planet.

2. My BODY should be preserved.

3. My BODY requires daily attention.

4. My BODY prospers when I feed it, exercise it, and give it proper rest.

5. My BODY works for me when I respect its needs.

6. My BODY, when healthy, allows me to work.

7. My BODY should not be overworked.

8. My BODY enjoys being touched: hugs, affection, massage, sensual and sexual touch.

9. My BODY houses the spirit of the Divine.

10. My BODY is a gift from the Divine.

11. My BODY is Divine.

Calling

ONE OF THE QUESTIONS that often consumes an individual is "What should I do?" The real question to ask is not "What should I do?" but "Who am I?" When we begin to explore the self, we discover the golden treasure. When we consistently pay attention to what we enjoy doing so much that we would do it for free, then we begin to traverse the path that will reveal what it is we should do. We must get cozy with ourselves. The answer lies within.

POWER STATEMENTS

1. My CALLING is my primary work while on the planet.

2. My CALLING is at one with the life that I am living.

3. My CALLING is signaled by the throb of my heart.

4. My CALLING is recognized as I hear the Divine Word.

5. My CALLING is embraced as I follow the Word of the Divine.

6. My CALLING consistently and continually calls out to me.

7. My CALLING brings abundance as I let go of fear.

8. My CALLING blesses me as well as those that I serve.

9. My CALLING is acknowledged as others call me.

10. My CALLING says, "Answer the call."

11. I am CALLED.

Celebration

TO TAKE TIME OUT to do a ritual, perform a ceremony, or organize festivities saluting the culmination of an event should not be devalued. In Western culture, it is all about attaining more, yet how often do we celebrate what we have already attained? Do we evoke a conscious moment where we commune with the unseen spirit for our success? Do we understand that we do not have to wait for those big events (marriages, graduations, etc.) in life to occur before we celebrate? Acknowledge that each day you are alive there is something to celebrate.

POWER STATEMENTS

1. CELEBRATION is rejoicing because I have witnessed manifestation.

2. CELEBRATION is not just for special occasions, but for everyday accomplishments, too.

3. CELEBRATION takes place on special holidays, but every day is a holy day.

4. CELEBRATION of life should
not wait until my death; I will
celebrate while I am still alive.

5. CELEBRATION does not have to be a
huge public festivity; it can be a simple
act of thanks and expression of joy.

6. CELEBRATION brings merriment,
tears, laughter, and camaraderie.

7. CELEBRATION recognizes that something
that could have gone wrong did not occur.

8. CELEBRATION reminds me of the
goodness of the Divine.

9. CELEBRATION is appropriate at
the end of each day.

10. CELEBRATION is giving thanks
for what I have.

11. CELEBRATION is vital.

Challenges

CHALLENGES PRESENT THEMSELVES to test our mental, emotional, and spiritual development. How we respond to challenges demonstrates our effectiveness in dealing with life's moments. Things are always happening. Sometimes we have to make things happen, while other times it is best to relax and let things happen around us. Whatever the case may be, we must consciously act, rather than emotionally react.

If you are at a complete loss as to what to do, it is appropriate to get other opinions. Process the challenge you're facing with a relative, friend, or expert. The challenging moment is a defining one, particularly as you experience the ramifications of how you deal with the challenge.

POWER STATEMENTS

1. CHALLENGES come and go.

2. CHALLENGES present themselves to keep me conscious of the Divine.

3. CHALLENGES are part of the play of the Divine.

4. CHALLENGES are merely moments in Time and Space.

5. CHALLENGES activate my intelligence, fortitude, and trust in myself.

6. CHALLENGES invigorate my adventuresome nature.

7. CHALLENGES are ameliorated when I face them head on.

8. CHALLENGES provoke me to consider possibilities.

9. CHALLENGES point me toward victory as I release doubt that I cannot overcome.

10. CHALLENGES go away when I am resourceful.

11. CHALLENGES remind me to have faith.

Meditation for

CALM

SIDDHA: *This is the meditation to do when you feel frenetic, neurotic, unfocused, and unclear. With conscious practice, you will become clear in mind and calm in spirit.*

Sit on the floor in easy pose, where your legs are crossed. This posture stills the energy of the lower centers of consciousness and allows us to more easily activate the higher centers of consciousness. You may also simply sit in a chair with your feet flat on the floor to ground yourself. Your spine should be straight and your neck an extension of your spine.

Now, bring the thumb of your right hand against the right nostril, completely closing it off so that you breathe through the left nostril. All the other fingers of your right hand should be pointing straight up. The left hand is in Gyan Mudra (thumb touches the tip of the Jupiter finger, the index finger) as it rests on the left thigh with the palm up or down.

Begin to breathe long, deep breaths through the left nostril. Focus on your breathing; if other thoughts come into your mind while this is happening, simply let them go and refocus on the breath coming in and going out. As you inhale, fill up the lower lungs, middle lungs, then upper lungs. As you exhale, exhale all the breath completely out of the lungs. Continue breathing through the left nostril. Practice this conscious rhythmic breathing for 3 to 11 minutes.

Children

CHILDREN ARE BORN FROM THE COSMOS to planet Earth to be nurtured and matured into adults. Yet, it is we, their adult caretakers, who are responsible for their safety, education, and emotional well-being. Children are new. They are our legacy as well as our future.

POWER STATEMENTS

1. CHILDREN come from the unknown.

2. CHILDREN are gifts that should be cared for by the people around them.

3. CHILDREN learn from adults and other children.

4. CHILDREN can teach the adults around them.

5. CHILDREN grow.

6. CHILDREN blossom with attention.

7. CHILDREN require my attention.

8. CHILDREN should be guided.

9. CHILDREN have vast potential.

10. CHILDREN that are cared for now will excel in the future.

11. CHILDREN bring great delight.

Choice

CHOICES ARE THE DECISIONS WE MAKE FROM MOMENT TO MOMENT, yet how efficacious our choices will be depends on whether they are in alignment with the Divine. It is when we consciously commit to doing our daily spiritual work, emotional cleansing, and mental focusing that our choices will be unconsciously conscious (meaning that we will make the best choice without conscious thought). It is then that we will overstep the landmines that can devastate our personal, relational, financial, and familial lives.

POWER STATEMENTS

1. CHOICE gives me infinite possibilities.

2. CHOICE invigorates my life.

3. CHOICE must be made in the moment.

4. CHOICE will be rooted in
    compassion for self and others.

5. CHOICE has consequences.

6. CHOICE impacts my future.

7. CHOICE should enhance my freedom,
    strengthen my mental and emotional
    being, and do no harm to self or others.

8. CHOICE illuminates my path
    with good health, wholesome
    relationships, and a secure future.

9. CHOICE resulting from devoted
    spiritual work will cause my decisions
    to be unconsciously conscious.

10. CHOICE that is in alignment with the
    Divine will bring propitious results.

11. CHOICE is mine.

Clarity

IF I HAD BUT ONE WISH, it would be to have clarity. To have a clear understanding of what is happening in life with all its vicissitudes would be, unquestionably, comforting. If we had greater clarity, perhaps our lives would have fewer misgivings, mishaps, missed opportunities. It would assist us in making the best decisions as life presents its invitations, challenges, and temptations.

An excellent way to develop clarity is to meditate daily. Meditation is the worthy practice that will rid the unconscious of its mental debris (doubts, fears, insecurities) and bestow us with clarity. Throughout *The Pocket Guru* there are 11 meditations. Choose one or two to practice daily as clarity is heightened.

POWER STATEMENTS

1.   CLARITY guides and protects me.

2.   CLARITY comes when I seek
     the wisdom of others.

3.   CLARITY asks me to be fully conscious
     of the consequences of my actions.

4.   CLARITY steers me away from
     doing something I will regret.

5.   CLARITY tells me to take care of
     the details within my life.

6.   CLARITY comes when I acknowledge
     the longings of my heart.

7.   CLARITY is fueled by daily
     spiritual practice.

8.   CLARITY comes when I am peaceful.

9.   CLARITY becomes peace when I merge
     with the rhythm of my breath.

10. CLARITY comes when I listen from
     the still, quiet space inside.

11. CLARITY.

Commitment

AN INDIVIDUAL who has the ability to commit is to be respected and valued. A person who cannot commit is not wholly trustworthy. Indeed, if a person cannot commit to their word, then they also cannot commit to a wholesome relationship, even a wholesome relationship with themselves. When we do commit to ourselves, that means we are committed to our passions, likes, dislikes, and feelings. Our heart is committed to not missing a beat; our breath is committed to keeping us alive. Allow us to be as committed to ourselves as the Divine is committed to us.

In addition, we have to learn to commit to our personal ideation and goals; otherwise we are creating a situation in which the universe will not be committed to fulfilling those goals. We get not what we want in life but that to which we commit. It is our commitment that will bring about the things of the world that we seek.

POWER STATEMENTS

1. COMMITMENT is a conscious choice.

2. COMMITMENT does not waver.

3. COMMITMENT is always doing
    what I said I would do.

4. COMMITMENT sustained creates
    trust from others.

5. COMMITMENT is deciding to be
    one of the best at what I do.

6. COMMITMENT is necessary
    to reach my goals.

7. COMMITMENT added to
    intuition equals success.

8. COMMITMENT to principles of Higher
    Consciousness gains me respect.

9. COMMITMENT to righteousness will
    bring the right things to me.

10. COMMITMENT overcomes fate and
    propels me toward my destiny.

11. COMMITMENT is the way to
    a prosperous future.

Communication

COMMUNICATION IS ONE OF THOSE ELEMENTS in life that is central to harmonious relationships and pleasant outcomes. And something that assuredly enhances communication is the awareness that communication is heart to heart, not head to head.

Communication is not to be viewed as an attempt to convince someone of something. It is to be viewed as connecting to someone else's heartfelt perspective as you share your thoughts. Take a good look at to whom you are speaking. What are they feeling? See the world through their eyes as you speak to their heart from your heart; that is how a meeting of the minds will result.

POWER STATEMENTS

1. COMMUNICATION is essential in maintaining relationships.

2. COMMUNICATION can overcome a rupture in a relationship.

3. COMMUNICATION is never to disrespect or abuse another.

4.   COMMUNICATION is enhanced as
     I actively listen to others.

5.   COMMUNICATION requires me to
     consciously choose my words.

6.   COMMUNICATION is verbal and nonverbal.

7.   COMMUNICATION connects me to
     my friends, relatives, intimate
     others, and children.

8.   COMMUNICATION sustains camaraderie
     among my family members, coworkers,
     and community.

9.   COMMUNICATION is about hearing
     not just words, but also needs.

10. COMMUNICATION requires that I
     feel myself as well as the other.

11. COMMUNICATION is heart to
     heart, not head to head.

Compassion

IT IS ALWAYS ENDEARING to see and hear stories of someone who selflessly served another. It warms the heart to witness or hear of someone who lived in their heart and was kind to another.

POWER STATEMENTS

1. COMPASSION means first and foremost being kind and considerate to myself.

2. COMPASSION is the caring that guides my words and actions.

3. COMPASSION is being the good luck in the midst of another's bad luck.

4. COMPASSION is giving and sharing with others who are less fortunate.

5. COMPASSION allows me to forgive another when they have transgressed against me.

6. COMPASSION overrides my sense of pain and anger.

7. COMPASSION does not permit vengeance.

8. COMPASSION allows me to maintain my grace and dignity as I acknowledge the Divine in others.

9. COMPASSION means not judging another as right or wrong, good or bad.

10. COMPASSION comes from my purity, which is the Divine within.

11. COMPASSION places me in the realm of Higher Consciousness.

Completion

IT IS ABOUT FINISHING THE RACE. If we start something, then finish it and, above all, do our best. If we are having trouble completing a task, it is absolutely appropriate to seek help. Tasks done with the help of a team are no less important than ones we complete without outside assistance.

First thing in the morning, jot down the projected tasks to be completed that day, and if you do not complete them, put them on your list for the following day. Do the same for tasks that take place over the course of a week, month, or year, and check in to see how you are accomplishing them. Relish in the moment when you can scratch those tasks off your list as you complete them. Finish what you start.

POWER STATEMENTS

1. COMPLETION is the goal.

2. COMPLETION is achieved with unwavering focus.

3. COMPLETION comes with determination to make it to the finish line.

4. COMPLETION is mine as I perpetually put one foot in front of the other.

5. COMPLETION is pleasurable when I decide to enjoy the process.

6. COMPLETION takes time.

7. COMPLETION says, "Take a rest, but then get back on the horse."

8. COMPLETION tells me I have done my best.

9. COMPLETION heightens my self-esteem.

10. COMPLETION is to be celebrated.

11. COMPLETION says, "Job well done, now on to the next."

Confidence

IT IS A WORTHY FOCUS to develop the art and science of saying what we feel, feeling what we say, and saying what we see. For us to have confidence, we must come into a relationship with strength, honesty, and love as we embrace reality in a dignified way. No one can live for us and no one can die for us. So, when the day comes that we decide to live our lives in a fully embodied manner, then we will have displayed confidence.

POWER STATEMENTS

1. CONFIDENCE lives inside me.

2. CONFIDENCE tells me, "I am enough."

3. CONFIDENCE lets me know that I am deserving.

4. CONFIDENCE tells me to speak from my heart.

5. CONFIDENCE empowers me to effectively speak my truth.

6. CONFIDENCE tells me to love the life I am living.

7. CONFIDENCE spurs courage.

8. CONFIDENCE gives me courage to do what I must do to be happy.

9. CONFIDENCE inspires me to live my best life.

10. CONFIDENCE says, "Go for it."

11. CONFIDENCE is mine.

Control

EVERYONE WANTS TO BE IN CONTROL; yet to have a realistic understanding of this concept is to know that we can control only our own behavioral choices. We do not have control over others. And we most definitely do not have control over Mother Nature. The awareness of our vulnerability and lack of control can create angst and existential anxiety.

In merging with the Divine during meditative practice, our oneness is enhanced as we are intuitively guided to be in the right place at the right time, doing and saying the right thing. In relating to what is in absolute control through meditation, the practitioner eventually gains control.

POWER STATEMENTS

1. CONTROL of my mental and emotional balance comes through devoted meditative practice.

2. CONTROL of my emotional reactions is vital to harmonious relationships.

3. CONTROL of my emotional reactions comes when I utilize unsettling moments as an opportunity to display my grace.

4. CONTROL of my words is important when speaking to another.

5. CONTROL of my environment comes through being organized.

6. CONTROL is the art and science of managing my life.

7. CONTROL is mine as I relinquish the idea of trying to control another.

8. CONTROL comes when I meditate and listen to the talk of the Divine.

9. CONTROL is mine in knowing the Divine is arranging my affairs.

10. CONTROL means knowing that the Divine is always in control.

11. CONTROL is gained through meditation with the Divine, which has absolute control.

Meditation to
INCREASE ENERGY

SIDDHA: *This is a meditation to do when one is depressed and low on energy. The right side of the body is the masculine side of the body, the sun side. Breathing through the right nostril will enhance mental focus.*

Sit on the floor in easy pose, where your legs are crossed. This posture stills the energy of the lower centers of consciousness and allows us to more easily activate the higher centers of consciousness. You may also simply sit in a chair with your feet flat on the floor to ground yourself. Your spine should be straight and your neck an extension of your spine.

Now, bring the thumb of your left hand against your left nostril, completely closing it off so that you breathe through the right nostril. All the other fingers of your left hand should be pointing straight up. Begin to breathe long and deep through the right nostril. The right hand is in Gyan Mudra (see page 33) as it rests on the right thigh with the palm up or down. Focus on your breathing; if thoughts come into your mind while this is happening, simply let them go and refocus on the breath coming in and going out. As you inhale, fill up the lower lungs, middle lungs, then upper lungs. As you exhale, exhale completely. Continue breathing through the right nostril. Practice this conscious rhythmic breathing for 3 to 11 minutes.

Courage

ALL GREAT PEOPLE throughout history have needed courage to push through in the face of obstacles, persevere through the onslaught of negativity, and battle with odds that seemed impossible to overcome. To have courage does not mean to lack fear; it means not succumbing to that fear. We can be fearful, but we must proceed forward anyway. We will never succeed without steadfast courage to keep going.

POWER STATEMENTS

1. COURAGE walks through fear.

2. COURAGE is employed by the fearless warrior.

3. COURAGE allows me to overcome obstacles.

4. COURAGE convinces me that I can overcome odds.

5. COURAGE is the fire that blazes my path.

6. COURAGE is my will in action.

7. COURAGE propels me to speak honestly.

8. COURAGE helps me achieve possibility.

9. COURAGE knows my potential.

10. COURAGE helps me reach my highest potential.

11. COURAGE stands proud and proclaims victory.

Creativity

WE ALL HAVE THE ABILITY to create, for we are at one with the Divine, the Infinite Creative Consciousness; therefore, we have the ability to be infinitely creative.

POWER STATEMENTS

1.   CREATIVITY is my privilege; otherwise, boredom, stagnation, and lack seep in.

2.   CREATIVITY can break boredom in my day-to-day routine.

3.   CREATIVITY is the play of the child.

4.   CREATIVITY takes place at home, at work, and within the world at large.

5.   CREATIVITY goes through stages as I embrace the process.

6.   CREATIVITY sometimes requires the input of others.

7.   CREATIVITY is bringing the unseen into concrete vision and making the unspoken audible.

8.   CREATIVITY is a process of surrendering to the universal mind as ideas come.

9.   CREATIVITY tells me to sit quietly and imagine.

10. CREATIVITY allows me to invent.

11. CREATIVITY inspires.

Death

IN THE EARLIER STAGES OF LIFE, we may erroneously think that everyone will die but us. That denial can work for a while, but when it is time for the soul to leave the physical body, hopefully we will have lived! Death will, assuredly come to us all; it is a reminder to live our lives with gusto.

POWER STATEMENTS

1.   DEATH lives.

2.   DEATH is a part of life.

3.   DEATH sometimes surprisingly appears.

4.   DEATH is the unseen that will take
     me into the unknown.

5.   DEATH can be a peaceful transformation
     when life is lived consciously.

6.   DEATH is the absence of movement.

7.   DEATH is the transmigration of the soul.

8.   DEATH is not on my mind
     when I find purpose.

9.   DEATH reminds me to keep moving.

10. DEATH alerts me to the
     importance of today.

11. DEATH reminds me to do
     what I enjoy now.

Decisions

WE MAKE DECISIONS every second of the day. Even procrastination is a decision, for we are deciding not to move. In making a decision, we should always consider the consequences of that choice. Will our decisions harm ourselves or others? Will they prosper our personal growth and development? Will they help us achieve our life goals? And that which is most important: Will we be acting in the realm of Higher Consciousness, so we do not reap negative karma (a universal law which denotes that for every action, there is an equal and opposite reaction)?

POWER STATEMENTS

1. DECISIONS are made by all
   peoples of the world.

2. DECISIONS have been made by others;
   now I must make a conscious decision.

3. DECISIONS impact my relationships.

4. DECISIONS should be thought through
   for possible consequences.

5. DECISIONS can alter my path
   for better or for worse.

6. DECISIONS can heal situations.

7. DECISIONS made wisely
   can improve my life.

8. DECISIONS made wisely can
   enhance my physical security.

9. DECISIONS made wisely can
   secure my future.

10. DECISIONS made wisely put me at ease.

11. DECISIONS bring me peace of mind.

Depression

DEPRESSION FEELS AS IF we have been pulled into the Underworld, away from light into the darkness of despair. How are we to live through this descent? Can we be careful not to literalize—make tangible to the point of being a living entity—the depression and identify with it to such an extent that we entertain harm to ourselves? To successfully navigate through despair requires being careful not to judge it or resist it. It is there for a reason.

But what is the reason? Have we had a recent loss? Have we received some unsettling news? Are we failing to take care of our needs and feeling worn down? Is there a chemical imbalance that would incline us to seek help from a medical professional? Or are we spiritually depleted?

Our depression is asking us to let it be while it provokes us to a new consciousness, new thoughts, and a new way of doing and being in the world. We may retreat if we must, but we should take time to acknowledge the descent and allow for the emergence of inspiration. We are in a very, very powerful place for a new creativity.

To alleviate depression, can we have a cathartic moment by watching a depressing movie or an uplifting one? Can we make an opening for the depression to speak aloud as we draw, write, dance, or talk it out? These are all means by which we can get out of our depression by getting into it.

The spiritual component is also important. Is it time to elevate the spirit and meditate? We must reignite the spirit daily. Get your day going by starting it with a morning meditative practice. Depression does not have to be a permanent state of being. Identify it and let it inform you as to what is being asked of you.

POWER STATEMENTS

1. DEPRESSION suffocates my life.

2. DEPRESSION lives and life stagnates.

3. DEPRESSION is pressing my spirit down.

4. DEPRESSION happens.

5. DEPRESSION can go away.

6. DEPRESSION provokes me to ask, "Why am I depressed?"

7.   DEPRESSION is diminished as I
     reach out to friends, relatives,
     therapists, ministers, healers.

8.   DEPRESSION is lessened when
     I take better care of my body
     and begin to exercise.

9.   DEPRESSION can be alleviated when
     I dance, write, paint, and find other
     ways to express my emotions.

10. DEPRESSION asks me to meditate
     to connect to my soul.

11. DEPRESSION subsides when I do long
     deep breathing for 11 minutes.

Deserve

WE DO NOT GET WHAT WE WANT IN LIFE; we get what
we deserve. There is the understanding that everyone
should respect us, love us, and, assuredly, pay us well.
Unfortunately, that does not automatically happen.
We must acknowledge and proclaim our self-worth.
There is something powerful about fully accepting
ourselves and knowing that something is rightfully
ours. It is in that consciousness that the possibility of getting not only what we want but what we
deserve will come.

POWER STATEMENTS

1. I DESERVE to dream my life;
   I will work for it.

2. I DESERVE the privilege of working
   to become a better individual.

3. I DESERVE responsible teachers.

4. I DESERVE to be compensated as
   befits my skill set and experience.

5. I DESERVE to be myself while I
   consciously respect others.

6. I DESERVE to be respected.

7. I DESERVE to have my physical,
   emotional, and mental needs met.

8. I DESERVE family members and
   intimate companions who express
   their love and appreciation for me.

9. I DESERVE love.

10. I DESERVE to be happy.

11. I DESERVE.

Destruction

DESTRUCTION IS COMMONLY not welcomed for it usually evokes sadness. Is our pain in any way assuaged through an understanding that from destruction comes rebirth? Allow us to embrace the reality that destruction will continue to occur, for it is part of Divine evolution.

POWER STATEMENTS

1. DESTRUCTION is part of the Divine, although it is still hard to fathom.

2. DESTRUCTION can sometimes be offset when I follow my intuition.

3. DESTRUCTION feels like a death.

4. DESTRUCTION occurs, and sometimes I simply must witness so that I can learn and move on.

5. DESTRUCTION says it's time to change and let go.

6. DESTRUCTION occurs so that reconstruction of my life can begin.

7. DESTRUCTION is an opportunity to rebuild and realign.

8. DESTRUCTION creates a vacuum for something new to fill the space.

9. DESTRUCTION is a stage in the creative process.

10. DESTRUCTION is part of the journey of the personal and universal soul.

11. DESTRUCTION no longer disillusions me.

Discipline

WOULD IT NOT BE GREAT if we could learn the arts, sciences, and systems of thought simply through the process of osmosis? Unfortunately, this is not the case. In order to learn, we must do the work and we must keep doing the work until we have mastered it. That is discipline. This is the foundation for achievement. Discipline requires mental focus and a physical commitment.

POWER STATEMENTS

1. DISCIPLINE must be practiced daily.

2. DISCIPLINE confronts the limitations of my ego.

3. DISCIPLINE is strengthened with heartfelt passion.

4. DISCIPLINE is developing good habits.

5. DISCIPLINE will enhance my skill set.

6. DISCIPLINE will enhance my health, emotional well-being, and career security.

7. DISCIPLINE results in a good reputation, enhanced financial revenue, and recognition of services.

8. DISCIPLINE is key to climbing the mountain and making sure I stay on top.

9. DISCIPLINE says, "Stay on course."

10. DISCIPLINE is doing the work.

11. DISCIPLINE is the work of the master.

Disease

DISEASE, AS A SYMPTOM, is a key to the cure. What part of our body is asking for our attention? Our lungs? Then perhaps we are not breathing life and fully living. Our back? Perhaps we are not getting the support that we need. The kidneys? The kidneys relate to water, and on an emotional, mental, and spiritual level, that means sadness is in the being—there are tears that need to flow.

If we look at disease as an opportunity to expand and correct emotional, mental, and spiritual imbalances, then we are setting in motion the possibility of healing. Disease is telling us that we are out of balance. How can we restore the balance? This is our opportunity to push the reset button.

POWER STATEMENTS

1.   DISEASE alerts me to restore
     balance in my life.

2.   DISEASE inspires me to
     confer with experts.

3.   DISEASE begins to leave when I start
     being compassionate with myself.

4.   DISEASE asks me to be present to
     my needs, longings, and fears.

5.   DISEASE pushes me to work through my
     feelings and sit in a neutrality of being.

6.   DISEASE says, "Express my feelings."

7.   DISEASE tells me to slow down
     and spend time with myself.

8.   DISEASE says, "Be patient."

9.   DISEASE suggests that I change my habits.

10. DISEASE is an opportunity to
     process my life choices.

11. DISEASE is my chance to heal
     my life, not just my body.

Meditation for
MENTAL ALERTNESS

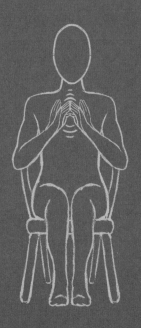

SIDDHA: *Do this meditation when you feel brain-dead. This meditation will stimulate your mind. You will feel more mentally alert.*

———————●———————

Sit in easy pose, where your legs are crossed, or comfortably in a chair with your feet flat on the floor. Your spine should be straight and your neck an extension of your spine. With your fingers spread, bring both hands up to the level of the heart chakra. The palms of the hands are facing each other. Begin to rhythmically hit the pads of the fingertips of the opposite hands together. Throughout the meditation, breathe long and deep. Do this rhythmic motion of tapping the fingertips with those of the opposite hand for 3 to 5 minutes.

⧖ Divine

WHEN AN INDIVIDUAL sees the Divine as omnipresent, then that individual is in relationship to Higher Consciousness. The victory, the defeat, the accident, the challenge—all of it, is the Divine! To begin our day by giving homage to the Divine in our particular way, and thinking about and feeling the Divine's presence all day, is to be in a constant relationship and ever-present with the Divine.

Even still, there are several ways to relate to the Divine. We can think of the Divine as mother, father, lover, or friend. I, personally, think of the Divine as a mother who is ever compassionate, even when I make a slip. However, one can relate to the Divine as the father, which is rather common within cultures where the Divine is perceived as a protecting, guiding force. The Divine, the father, will also discipline us and give us a reminder that perhaps we should not do that again. Yet, if we think of the Divine as our lover, we will know beyond a doubt that, no matter what is happening, love is there. For example, getting laid off from a job is, initially, not received as a pleasant experience until we realize the good that will have ensued (e.g., time to be with loved ones, finally time to do what we really enjoy, a better job in the future, and so on). This orientation to the Divine embodies the frequent statement, "The Divine is love." But when we see the Divine as our friend, then we can rest assured that whatever mishap has occurred, assistance will come, the advice will come, the money will come. The Divine, our friend, will send someone or something to help us get out of the mess that we are in. Choose one of these perspectives and begin living a life that is Divine.

POWER STATEMENTS

1. The DIVINE is all that I can imagine, feel, hear, touch, and taste.

2. The DIVINE gives me time and space to grow and prosper.

3. The DIVINE is the Alpha and the Omega and everything in between.

4. The DIVINE is in the space.

5. The DIVINE is timeless and spaceless.

6. The DIVINE is the seen and the unseen.

7. The DIVINE is waiting to be known.

8. The DIVINE is also unknown.

9. The DIVINE is within you.

10. The DIVINE is within me.

11. The DIVINE is.

Earth

THERE ARE OTHER PLANETS in the galaxy, but we are on planet Earth, a material plane where we walk and talk, fueled by the breath of life and ignited by the soul. We all inhabit the Earth for a relatively short time, considering that the universe has been in existence for billions of years. Make the best of your time while here. If you don't enjoy your stay, you will miss out.

POWER STATEMENTS

1. On planet EARTH, I live.

2. On planet EARTH, I live to love.

3. On planet EARTH, I consciously decide to live a life devoted to acts of caring toward animals, plants, self, and other.

4. On planet EARTH, I breathe, eat, drink, and eliminate.

5. On planet EARTH, which is like a hotel, I check in and, one day, I will check out.

6. On planet EARTH, I have free will.

7. On planet EARTH, destruction, drama, and dread sometimes occur.

8. On planet EARTH, I must utilize my consciousness to restore mental and emotional balance when rupture does occur.

9. On planet EARTH, I am subject to karmic reactions.

10. On planet EARTH, I thrive when I commit.

11. On planet EARTH, my etheric self— my spirit—is encased in a body.

Education

WE ALL NEED EDUCATION. We all must learn the culture and mores of our society. What are the rules? What is it that we must learn to thrive? I use the word *education* broadly, as I am not speaking of the necessity of going to college, but rather of being a student of life. Whether we learn from a mentor or on our own, it is necessary to be armed with knowledge that can help us succeed on our journey of life.

POWER STATEMENTS

1. EDUCATION comes when I am
    open to receive knowledge.

2. EDUCATION is for the young and the old.

3. EDUCATION assists me in the
    process of becoming myself.

4. EDUCATION means learning
    from the learned.

5. EDUCATION can come through
    formal schooling.

6. EDUCATION sometimes results in
    the reception of certifications,
    licenses, and degrees.

7. EDUCATION can come through
    having life experiences and
    carefully processing them.

8. EDUCATION assists me in
    becoming one of the learned.

9. EDUCATION continues throughout my life.

10. EDUCATION helps me master my life.

11. I welcome EDUCATION.

Ego

SO OFTEN, WE PATHOLOGIZE the ego. It is merely our identity of self. We have a healthy relationship with our ego when we are confidently and authentically ourselves. When we project ourselves as more (inflation of the self) or less (depreciation of the self) than we are, the impact of both is negative. The goal is to be centered as we accurately assess our limitations as well as our assets. We need our ego; we just need it to be in union with the Divine—then we will be at one. And we achieve this as we dedicatedly devote time to meditation, which will bring us into that Divine harmony.

POWER STATEMENTS

1. My EGO is my identity, my
    attachment, my limit.

2. My EGO is comforted by familiarity
    and fears the unknown.

3. My EGO, when fear based, resists change.

4. My EGO, when fear based, hampers
    my personal growth.

5. My EGO is negative when I project myself
    as more than I am or less than I am.

6. My EGO is negative if I succumb to hubris.

7. My EGO is positive when I inspire others.

8. My EGO, when in union with the Divine,
    results in peace and manifestation.

9. My EGO, when at one with the Divine,
    allows me to effectively interact with
    others in my environment.

10. My EGO empowers me to draw
    goodness into my life.

11. My EGO, when in union with the
    Divine, brings harmony.

Faith

FAITH LIVES when we embrace hope; however, if our relationship with spirituality is undeveloped, then it is hard to have faith. So, in order to have faith, one must open up to spirit, energy, the unseen. Every day, we must start with the awareness that yesterday we had faith that we would get up, and, obviously, we did. We must proceed throughout the day with faith that our affairs will be taken care of. Live, love, and surrender to the flow of life. Things are always happening around us. We are not in complete control. Trust in that flow and have faith.

POWER STATEMENTS

1. FAITH is an elevated state of hope.

2. FAITH is trust in the unknown.

3. FAITH is the whisper telling me to trust.

4. FAITH revealed herself to me,
   and she was real.

5. FAITH erodes my fear and
   heightens my love.

6. FAITH lives when I let go of
   fear and become neutral.

7. FAITH tells me to sit still and let
   things move around me.

8. FAITH shines when I bow my head
   and merge in love.

9. FAITH is coming to me.

10. FAITH is here.

11. FAITH.

Family

HOW IS A FAMILY CREATED? It is possible to marry into a family, be adopted into a family, or create our own community family (e.g., our crew, our buddies, our posse). Whatever the case may be, family is a group of people with whom we have a deep and abiding connection, whether through bloodline or not. And even though we are a family, conflicts and disagreements occur. The goal is how to sustain the family camaraderie. The family is at its best when there's cooperation among family members.

POWER STATEMENTS

1. FAMILY members are sometimes blood relatives and sometimes not.

2. FAMILY members and I share the idea of "we," even though we individually differ.

3. FAMILY members sometimes disappoint and upset me.

4. FAMILY members inspire me to forgive.

5. FAMILY members are my tribe.

6. FAMILY members inspire me to learn how to communicate to resolve conflicts.

7. FAMILY members care for each other enough to share their feelings.

8. FAMILY members live in peace, sometimes in conflict, but always in love.

9. FAMILY members come together to learn to love.

10. FAMILY members live love and let live.

11. FAMILY members live.

Father

THERE IS THE MOTHER and there is the father; both are important. Praise be to the father, whether he is biological, adopted, grandfather, or stepfather. It is his words and actions that guide us to know that we are strong and powerful. The "good enough" father provides stability and dependability.

POWER STATEMENTS

1.   FATHER we may see as a god,
     but he is human.

2.   FATHER can abandon me or provide a
     stable, dependable environment.

3.   FATHER who lacks emotional
     intelligence impacts my ability to
     deeply connect with another.

4.   FATHER sets an example of
     strength and security.

5.   FATHER who sacrifices lets me know
     I am worthy of love.

6.   FATHER impacts my clarity of purpose.

7.   FATHER transmits reassurance
     through his touch.

8.   FATHER gives me confidence when
     he takes time to listen to me.

9.   FATHER does his best; the latter
     part of life, I must do the rest.

10. FATHER can be a source of protection.

11. FATHER empowers my life.

Fear

ALL FEAR IS NOT IRRATIONAL. To see a rattlesnake and stand still until it passes is to have acted appropriately. Yet, when our fears are irrational and debilitating, we must learn to eliminate them from our psyche.

When we find ourselves in a place where fear is stunting our personal growth, then it is time to confront that fear and work through it mentally and emotionally. Extreme fear turns into anxiety, which can in turn lead to panic attacks and a myriad of moments within our lives where we are stunted/paralyzed. To release undue fear takes concentrated work as we unearth deeply rooted repressed feelings. The following mantras will assist you in eradicating debilitating fears.

POWER STATEMENTS

1. FEAR limits me.

2. FEAR can paralyze.

3. FEAR can alert me to possible danger.

4. FEAR is sometimes a mirage, which befools me.

5. FEAR goes away when I overcome irrationality.

6. FEAR can bond like-minded people, for better or worse.

7. FEAR can be a catalyst to motivate me into action.

8. FEAR can be a wake-up call to change my life.

9. FEAR goes away when transmuted into love.

10. FEAR can activate my courage and bravery.

11. FEAR less.

Feelings

FEELINGS MAY NOT BE LOGICAL, but, nonetheless, they are real. Feelings are energy moving through us to inform us what is transpiring within the depth of our being. To not acknowledge our feelings is to disrespect ourselves. To deny our feelings is to be shut down to an energy that can propel personal growth.

Learn to express your feelings so that they do not turn into dark energy that can cause disease. On a holistic level, disease is simply a symptom that encourages you to process parts of yourself that you have ignored. Feelings are not something to devalue. Devalue feelings and simultaneously you devalue the self. Say what you feel and feel what you say, and then you will be at one.

POWER STATEMENTS

1. My FEELINGS are real.

2. My FEELINGS are not always comfortable, but all of them are good.

3.   My FEELINGS are uncomfortable when
my head and heart are in conflict.

4.   My FEELINGS are never wrong; my head
must intelligently guide me as to what to
do, creating no harm to self or others.

5.   My FEELINGS must be supported
by my head so that I am at one.

6.   My FEELINGS are the fuel
that propel my growth.

7.   My FEELINGS give me a deep
understanding of myself in the moment.

8.   My FEELINGS, when acknowledged and
expressed, show I am respecting myself.

9.   My FEELINGS, when consistently
acknowledged, allow me to
feel others' feelings.

10.   My FEELINGS should always
be effectively expressed.

11.   My FEELINGS, when effectively
expressed, bring fulfillment.

Meditation to

DEVELOP THE
HEART CHAKRA

SIDDHA: *This meditation will bring you into a heartfelt relationship with self and others. You will begin to process life from the perspective of heart (e.g., warmth, compassion, empathy). It will enhance your ability to speak heart to heart with another individual. Your words will resonate in the hearts of others.*

Sit on the floor in easy pose where your legs are crossed. This posture stills the energy of the lower centers of consciousness and allows us to more easily activate the higher centers of consciousness. You may also simply sit in a chair with your feet flat on the floor to ground yourself. Your spine should be straight and your neck an extension of your spine.

Crisscross the hands, palms touching the chest, the sternum, the heart chakra. Begin to breathe long and deep as you bring your consciousness to the center of your chest. Experience the sensations at this center. After 2 minutes of long deep breathing, begin to chant the mantra, *I feel, I feel myself, I am, I am*. Let the mind merge with what you are saying. Chant this for 11 minutes.

Feminine Principle

THERE IS THE DIVINE, which has differentiated itself into two operating forces: the Feminine Principle and the Masculine Principle. They are polarities of consciousness; neither is better than the other, simply different.

The Feminine Principle is akin to the moon: It is changeable and has phases. It is never the same. It is ever moving. The Feminine Principle is supportive, as it revolves around others. It is the energetic force, the creative unit, and the nurturer of life.

POWER STATEMENTS

1. FEMININE PRINCIPLE is embodied in both woman and man.

2. FEMININE PRINCIPLE is the Infinite Creative Consciousness.

3. FEMININE PRINCIPLE is light and dark just like the moon.

4. FEMININE PRINCIPLE is supportive like Mother Earth.

5. FEMININE PRINCIPLE is cyclical and seasonal like Mother Nature.

6. FEMININE PRINCIPLE is flowing and ever changeable.

7. FEMININE PRINCIPLE within an individual is romantic, nurturing, and sensitive.

8. FEMININE PRINCIPLE within an individual is suggestive, indirect, and subtle.

9. FEMININE PRINCIPLE calms.

10. FEMININE PRINCIPLE feeds.

11. FEMININE PRINCIPLE works in collaboration with Masculine Principle to create balance.

Food

FOOD IS A NECESSITY. We can overindulge in food when we use it as a means to soothe ourselves when we are emotionally wrought. To have a wholesome relationship with food, we must be careful that we do not overeat or undernourish ourselves. The yogic teaching is that eighty morsels of food make one drop of blood. This information lets us know that what we eat impacts our blood, which in turn goes to our brain, which in turn affects our behavior. There is truth in the adage "You are what you eat," so become conscious of what you put in your body. We have learned to eat for our taste, but perhaps we can begin to also eat for our health.

POWER STATEMENTS

1. FOOD sustains my life.

2. FOOD that is nutritious
   maintains my health.

3. FOOD gives me energy and strength.

4. FOOD is to be eaten when I'm hungry.

5. FOOD is to be savored and chewed,
   not gulped and swallowed down.

6. FOOD fuels my body and soothes my soul.

7. FOOD impacts my brain as well as my body.

8. FOOD determines how
   mentally conscious I am.

9. FOOD can elevate or depress my mood.

10. FOOD eaten with others is communion.

11. FOOD prepared consciously
    is love being eaten.

Forgiving

FORGIVING IS NOT EASY. We are human, and at times, for whatever reason, we feel we have been slighted. Allow us to acknowledge our feelings and process what transpired. Whatever the case may be, it is best to completely let go of resentment, for that will harm us in the future. Resentment allowed to fester can later transform into physical unwellness. Rather than judge the individual who has violated our boundaries or our sense of good, give them to the Divine. In giving them to the Divine, we become completely resolved, as the spiritual law of karma becomes operative in the other's life. Resentment must go for the other as we perhaps must also forgive ourselves.

POWER STATEMENTS

1. FORGIVING another challenges my ego but uplifts my spirit.

2. FORGIVING I can do, but I forget only when my safety is not at risk.

3. FORGIVING another activates the process of transforming my hurt.

4. FORGIVING myself or another is essential, otherwise I mentally and emotionally stagnate.

5. FORGIVING myself or others reminds me that someone acted unconsciously.

6. FORGIVING involves looking at things from a broader perspective.

7. FORGIVING another triggers my awareness that all do not think or act like me.

8. FORGIVING myself or another can take time.

9. FORGIVING another catapults me into a realm of high spirituality.

10. FORGIVING another says, "Release and let go into love."

11. FORGIVING another frees me to love once again.

Friends

OH, TO HAVE REAL FRIENDS. Sometimes we meet someone and instantly bond, while other times a bond gradually deepens with someone we have met years ago, and we eventually declare ourselves friends. We are assisted on the journey of life when friends are around. Stay open and let them come. We can start perhaps by being a friend to ourselves as well as being friendly wherever we go. Just be ourselves. A friend likes us for who we are.

POWER STATEMENTS

1.   FRIENDS commune with me as we play, laugh, and cry together.

2.   FRIENDS help me during rough times.

3.   FRIENDS comfort me.

4.   FRIENDS relish in my spirit.

5.   FRIENDS make me feel alive.

6.   FRIENDS understand me.

7.   FRIENDS love me.

8.   FRIENDS teach me about myself.

9.   FRIENDS speak truth.

10. FRIENDS are my allies.

11. FRIENDS are coming to me now.

Fun

LET US ENDEAVOR to have fun in this life. In everything we do, allow us to find the joy, the amusement. In research that has focused on people on their deathbeds, one of the top regrets was not having enough fun. Let us begin to understand the importance of having fun.

POWER STATEMENTS

1. FUN is what I will have while living on the planet, so that on my deathbed I will have no regret.

2. FUN allows me to not always be so serious.

3. FUN asks me to sometimes break my mundane routine.

4. FUN is personal.

5. FUN is something I can experience while at work.

6. FUN is the focus of the child inside of me.

7. FUN is letting my spirit run free.

8. FUN is smiling, laughing, and feeling joy.

9. FUN is being with people who are committed to "release, relax, rejoice."

10. FUN is spending time with friends, children, lovers, family, and pets.

11. FUN is playful living.

Giving

GIVE FOR THE PURPOSE OF GIVING rather than with an expectation of receiving something in return. Learn to give from the heart, and you will inevitably learn to give unselfishly. When we give, we resonate with the Divine, the giver of life. Let us learn to give of our wisdom, time, skills, and even money, as the Divine will in turn give to us.

POWER STATEMENTS

1. GIVING is something I do from my heart.

2. GIVING is love being shared.

3. GIVING of my gifts is for those who are open to receive.

4. GIVING is something I can do when I have more than I need.

5. GIVING to those in need is an act of kindness.

6. GIVING selflessly endears others to me and pleases my soul.

7.   GIVING to others is reciprocated as the
     Divine, in turn, gives back to me.

8.   GIVING replicates the Divine,
     the giver of life.

9.   GIVING respite time to myself is
     an act of self-preservation.

10. GIVING unconditional love to myself
     empowers me to such an extent
     my presence attracts situations,
     people, and opportunities.

11. GIVING daily time for my spiritual
     work heightens my consciousness.

Greatest

GREAT! GREATER! GREATEST! What more than to be presented with principles that will make us aware and lighten our journey! The magnificence of it all!

Allow the following chapter verse to deepen us into nobility and eminence. Oh, to be illustrious! Oh, to live moment to moment in a conscious relationship with that which is the greatest.

POWER STATEMENTS

1. The GREATEST miracle is when I am blessed to come in contact with teachings of truth.

2. The GREATEST treachery is to turn my back on those teachings.

3. The GREATEST discipline is the practice of meditation to destroy duality of mind.

4. The GREATEST sacrifice is devoted nonattachment to misfortune, tragedy, and hardship.

5. The GREATEST love is when I selflessly give.

6. The GREATEST kindness is to be kind to those who have been unkind to me.

7. The GREATEST betrayal is to pollute my body and negate the longings of my heart.

8. The GREATEST gift is that of life.

9. The GREATEST truth is that one day I will die.

10. The GREATEST moment is when I realize that I am a manifestation of the Divine.

11. The GREATEST friend is the Divine.

Grit

WITHOUT GRIT—that internal determination and perseverance—our ability to complete projects and reach goals is almost nil. We need that drive, that unyielding thrust to go forward. We can have an idea in our head, but unless it is propelled by the passion of the spirited heart, chances of getting to the finish line are diminished. Ideas without the heartfelt passion to execute them will fall into the wasteland. How do we activate this force? See the goal, feel the passion, and keep up, until done!

POWER STATEMENTS

1. GRIT overcomes inertia.

2. GRIT destroys regrets.

3. GRIT tells me that if I can't run, keep walking.

4. GRIT never gives up.

5. GRIT stays focused on the goal.

6. GRIT keeps me going until my goal is reached.

7. GRIT allows me to make an impact on my environment.

8. GRIT makes things happen.

9. GRIT is the secret ingredient to my success.

10. GRIT is what distinguishes me as a champion.

11. GRIT belongs to me.

Happiness

HAPPINESS IS WHAT WE ALL DESIRE. We often look for it outside ourselves, in the perfect relationship, the ultimate job, or untold wealth. All those things can bring fulfillment but not real happiness. The real route to happiness is coming into harmony with the Divine. It is this oneness of self with the Divine that induces a joy and contentment as duality ceases. You will be happy, for you will be in harmony with the music of the spheres.

POWER STATEMENTS

1. HAPPINESS starts with the intention to be happy.

2. HAPPINESS comes when I feel worthy of being happy.

3. HAPPINESS is accompanied by an appreciation of myself.

4. HAPPINESS is felt with daily focus on fulfilling my needs.

5. HAPPINESS is a feeling.

6. HAPPINESS is living from my heart—that is rapture.

7. HAPPINESS is giving my worries to the Divine and letting things work themselves out.

8. HAPPINESS comes when I regularly meditate.

9. HAPPINESS is achieved when my mind, body, and soul are at one.

10. HAPPINESS is the simple joy of being.

11. HAPPINESS is here.

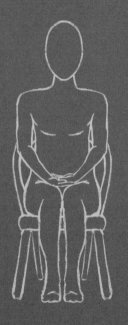

Meditation to
HEIGHTEN WISDOM

SIDDHA: *This is a simple meditation but very powerful in its impact. When practiced for 40 days, it will bring such a balance to the individual that they will flow harmoniously with others during interactions. The relationship with the Infinite Creative Consciousness will be heightened, as the ability to see creative solutions to situations and problematic circumstances will be further developed.*

Sit in a chair with your feet flat on the floor to ground yourself. Your spine should be straight and your neck an extension of your spine.

Now, place your right hand in the left hand, palms facing up. Have your eyes one-tenth open as you focus at the third eye, located at the root of the nose between the eyebrows. Inhale long and deep through the left nostril and exhale through the right nostril without touching the nose. Focus until you coordinate the breath. Practice this pranayama (conscious breath pattern) for 3 to 11 minutes.

Healing

DOCTORS DIAGNOSE, the Divine cures, but our consciousness heals. Within the spiritual world, the realm of infinite potentiality, disabilities and diseases can often miraculously heal. If our understanding and perception of the symptom is correct and we follow the Divine guidance, a healing can occur. Our personal consciousness is integral to healing.

POWER STATEMENTS

1. HEALING is possible.

2. HEALING puts a call out to the Divine.

3. HEALING takes time, but I
   will remain timeless.

4. HEALING is going into the pain
   and listening for guidance.

5. HEALING begins when I deepen
   into the reality that my symptom
   is the key to the cure.

6. HEALING encourages me to engage
   with the meaning of my symptom.

7. HEALING takes place when I have the
   right diagnosis and proper treatment.

8. HEALING is a process of re-envisioning
   my relationship to self and the world.

9. HEALING is getting clear about my
   real identity and purpose in life.

10. HEALING can occur when I am
    authentic and carefree.

11. HEALING activates my imagination
    of being whole.

Home

OUR HOME IS INTEGRAL to a peace of mind. Where do we feel safe? Some people live on the road, in trailers, condominiums, small family houses, mansions, cabins, or on a boat, while others have no permanent housing and continually move around. Some prefer to live alone, while others thrive when they live in a house full of people. The Pocket Guru hopes that all can maneuver life to such an extent that we find a living situation that feels like home.

POWER STATEMENTS

1. HOME is a place where I enjoy living.

2. HOME is the realization of what is in my mind's eye.

3. HOME environments change as I grow older.

4. HOME is a place where I have all my toys and "things" of the world that rejuvenate me.

5. HOME is clean and organized, and nurtures me for success.

6. HOME is necessary to have peace of mind.

7. HOME brings me peace, strength, and joy.

8. HOME is where I feed my body, calm my mind, and nourish my soul.

9. HOME is a place that I run to at the end of the day.

10. HOME is my place of refuge.

11. HOME is my sanctuary.

Hope

HOPE IS A DESIRE, a longing, a dream. Hope is the fire that keeps us striving and living with fervor. It is the act of making a request of the Divine and praying that the Divine delivers. Hope establishes a relationship with the future. As long as we are breathing, there is hope.

POWER STATEMENTS

1. HOPE is trust in the Divine.

2. HOPE overrides my fear.

3. HOPE transcends suffering.

4. HOPE recognizes my present situation while I dream the future.

5. HOPE is the vision I dare to dream.

6. HOPE is a vision I want to manifest.

7. HOPE is the frame of mind of champions.

8. HOPE is strengthened through prayer.

9. HOPE grows through loving thoughts.

10. HOPE energizes me to keep going.

11. HOPE makes life worth living.

Human

TO BE HUMAN is to understand that we have to work. We come into the world with talents and gifts and affinities, but to develop those attributes into assets that will help us throughout our lives, we must work. We must work in the spiritual, mental, and emotional arenas. We have weaknesses and we have strengths. There are spiritual laws and there are human laws. We live in between the two with the heartfelt goal of simply being ourselves and manifesting the excellence within.

POWER STATEMENTS

1. Being HUMAN means I must apply my consciousness to all situations.

2. Being HUMAN means that I am responsible for what comes in and goes out of my body.

3. Being HUMAN is knowing I must continue to work for personal growth.

4.   Being HUMAN is having a conscious
     balance between my concrete
     limitations and my vast potential.

5.   Being HUMAN is overcoming my
     weaknesses so that I can become
     the best rendition of myself.

6.   Being HUMAN is overcoming
     my fears, creating security, and
     continuing to move forward.

7.   Being HUMAN is having compassion
     for myself and others.

8.   Being HUMAN means that I may
     encounter enemies and challenges,
     but my inner light can overcome all.

9.   Being HUMAN is knowing that life
     is best when it is lovingly felt.

10. Being HUMAN is working to positively
     impact my world and the world at large.

11. Being HUMAN is knowing that the
     Divine dwells within me.

Humility

OF COURSE, we have the option to be prideful, yet, as many characters in myths and legends have learned, those who eschew humility meet terrible fates. Humility is knowing that we do not have absolute control within the universe and accepting that fact with grace. To engage in self-aggrandizement is not a worthy choice. Humility knows how to honor the Divine within self and others, as well as the all-encompassing Divine, which is beyond, unseen, and intangible.

POWER STATEMENTS

1. HUMILITY garners respect.

2. HUMILITY opposes hubris.

3. HUMILITY is achieved as I acknowledge that I am nothing, although I am one with that which is everything.

4. HUMILITY knows that I have concrete limitations yet vast potential, as the Divine is within me.

5.   HUMILITY is simultaneously
     knowing my power while knowing
     I am not all-powerful.

6.   HUMILITY becomes more pronounced
     the wiser I become.

7.   HUMILITY gives thanks for blessings
     bestowed throughout the day.

8.   HUMILITY is displayed as I honor
     the Divine in others.

9.   HUMILITY is embodied in my
     communication, as it is sensitive,
     heartfelt, and respectful.

10. HUMILITY shines through my
     refined and poised demeanor.

11. HUMILITY allows me to flow in grace.

"I" AM CUSTOM-MADE. There is no one like another. Each of us is unique. Your body and mind are yours and yours alone. The work is for us to live in our uniqueness. If we do not live our life with distinctiveness, then we forfeit the opportunity to relish in the glory of who we are. Not only will we sell ourselves short by not being our true selves, but others will be denied our special gifts and talents that we were placed here to share. Let us love ourselves, for we are part of the Divine.

POWER STATEMENTS

1. I CAN admire another, but
   I must master me.

2. I AM a unique creation of the Divine.

3. I STAY attuned to how I am,
   why I am, and that I am.

4. I AM already good, but I am working
   on being the best that I can be.

5. I USE my talents to uplift others
   as I do my spiritual, emotional,
   and mental work.

6. I AM kind.

7. I AM loving.

8. I AM emotionally intelligent
   and consistently developing
   my meditative mind.

9. I AM an example for others as
   I live a life of courage.

10. I TRUST myself.

11. I AM fully myself.

Ideas

IDEAS COME ALL THE TIME, yet which ones do we follow?

All ideas are not good ideas. Do not give any power to ideas that bear ill will or cause harm to self or others. If perchance we find ourselves pursuing an idea that will not reap good results for self and others, stop. Drop it. Choose to focus on other ideas. Continue to cleanse the subconscious mind through meditative practice.

POWER STATEMENTS

1. IDEAS are asking for my attention.

2. IDEAS beget other ideas.

3. IDEAS that come to me also
    come to another.

4. IDEAS are creative energy that
    have the potential to manifest.

5. IDEAS can become reality when
    I take courageous action.

6. IDEAS can create change.

7   IDEAS should be shared so others can
    help me bring them to fruition.

8. IDEAS should be tested and tried.

9. IDEAS sometimes seem incredible, but I
    will see if the Divine will support me.

10. IDEAS that come have chosen me.

11. IDEAS come from the Divine.

Intimacy

THE MAJORITY OF US have the desire to be intimate with another. Yet, to be truly intimate with another we must first become intimate with ourselves. Can we become intimate enough with ourselves so that we can be unguarded, even naked, with another? To find that intimacy we must deeply understand ourselves. What brings us joy? What are our passions? What displeases us? When we face our history, likes, and dislikes, then we are not only becoming intimate with ourselves but also positioning ourselves to become open and intimate with another.

POWER STATEMENTS

1. INTIMACY, I desire.

2. INTIMACY is a worthy goal.

3. INTIMACY begins as I become
    cozy with myself.

4. INTIMACY requires me to look
    at my past so that I can be
    understood in the present.

5. INTIMACY alerts me to what is
    and who is in my space.

6. INTIMACY with myself is necessary to
    have a real relationship with another.

7. INTIMACY will bring me close to some and
    reveal a need for space from others.

8. INTIMACY heightens my self-awareness.

9. INTIMACY relaxes me so that
    I can be myself.

10. INTIMACY asks me to deepen into
    unconditional self-love.

11. INTIMACY seduces me into
    truth and reality.

Intuition

WE DO NOT HAVE CLAWS like the tiger, a stench like the skunk, or quills like the porcupine. What we, as humans, primarily have to protect us is our intuition. Therefore, it would behoove us to develop the meditative mind so that our intuition can save us from transgressions, pitfalls, losses, failed collaborations, and destructive encounters.

Some situations, persons, and opportunities look good with two eyes, but when we develop and look through the third eye, that same situation may not look so good. As we discipline ourselves to consistently engage in meditative practice, we are developing a union with the Divine, and consequently more will become known to us.

POWER STATEMENTS

1. My INTUITION is the voice from the Divine.

2. My INTUITION is Divine guidance that I always follow so that I do not suffer.

3. My INTUITION prevents bad luck.

4. My INTUITION is sometimes scary but never wrong.

5. My INTUITION flows when I stop thinking and simply listen.

6. My INTUITION is increased when I quiet the voice of the ego with consistent meditation.

7. My INTUITION makes sense out of nonsense.

8. My INTUITION combined with my common sense leads me to the best decision.

9. My INTUITION brings order to my life.

10. My INTUITION tells me my role in life.

11. My INTUITION is transcendent knowledge.

Meditation to
CREATE MENTAL AND EMOTIONAL
BALANCE

SIDDHA: *This meditation brings the Masculine (right side) together with the Feminine (left side) to create centeredness in your being. You will then be able to interact in your environment from a neutral mindset. You will also find more effectiveness in your interactions, as this meditation heightens your sensitivity to self, others, and your environment.*

Sit on the floor in easy pose, where your legs are crossed. This posture stills the energy of the lower centers of consciousness and allows us to more easily activate the higher centers of consciousness. You may also simply sit in a chair with your feet flat on the floor to ground yourself. Your spine should be straight and your neck an extension of your spine. Bring the palms of your hands together, the right palm touching the left palm with your thumbs placed against the sternum of the chest. Thumbs should cross, as this neutralizes the ego. The rest of the fingers should be pointing at a 45-degree angle from the body. Begin to breathe long and deep, filling up the lower lungs, middle lungs, and upper lungs, and exhale completely. Slowly begin your practice of this meditation, starting with at least 3 minutes, working up to focusing your breath for a full 11 minutes.

Learn

LEARN, WE MUST. We can learn from a teacher, we can learn from our own experience, or we do not have to learn at all. Hopefully, we will not succumb to the path of not learning at all. A life where we are stubborn and resistant to growth results in limitation and repetitive experiences that do not serve us. Let us choose to learn and become one of the learned.

POWER STATEMENTS

1. I LEARN because the alternative is stagnation.

2. I LEARN both what to do and what not to do again.

3. I LEARN so that I can thrive.

4. I LEARN to access my talents and skills to cultivate abundant living.

5. I LEARN through reading.

6. I LEARN that the living universe is always communicating to me, if I but pay attention and process.

7. I LEARN from the people around me, consciously and unconsciously.

8. I LEARN when I study with a teacher.

9. I LEARN and eventually can become the teacher.

10. I LEARN, then I serve.

11. I LEARN, I practice, I evolve.

Lies

LYING CAN BE most detrimental to our success. The universe is built on truth. When we lie, we take ourselves out of alignment with Divine truth; as a result, success is compromised. If we tell lies, we weaken our impact, as the universe will not support our efforts. If we tell the truth, we come into harmony with the universe. If we tell the truth, we develop the ability to realize whatever we say. The latter is referred to as Vak Siddhi in spiritual texts.

POWER STATEMENTS

1. LIES compromise my success.

2. LIES can destroy trust when they
    are discovered to be untruths.

3. LIES derail me from having an honest
    relationship with another.

4. LIES are a betrayal to others
    as well as to myself.

5. LIES to myself make me inauthentic.

6. LIES denote fear of telling the truth.

7. LIES avoided help protect my reputation.

8. LIES give me a false sense of protection;
    they do not help but only hurt me.

9. LIES bring me out of alignment
    with the Divine universe.

10. LIES will not be told, for I have integrity.

11. LIES will not be told, as I will attain Vak
    Siddha—whatever I say will come true.

Life

JUST BECAUSE WE HAVE LIFE does not mean that there will always be good times. We will have challenges, turmoil, failures, losses; that is part of the life package. The best way of dealing with life is with an elevated consciousness. Therefore, it is the work that we do while on the planet to raise our consciousness that is time best spent. It is during prayerful times, meditation, reading spiritual literature, communing with nature, engaging in rituals to evoke the Divine, and moments of reverie that we will be enhancing our ability to consciously deal with everything that life brings to us. To be conscious, at all times, is most important, for it literally takes one second to make a decision that could have deleterious results. From this day onward allow ourselves to see life as an opportunity to be conscious.

POWER STATEMENTS

1. LIFE is to be lived.

2. LIFE presents opportunities, challenges, and tests.

3. LIFE is riding the wave.

4. LIFE is jumping the hurdle.

5. LIFE says, "Rest when you need to."

6. LIFE says, "Get back up and go."

7. LIFE is movement.

8. LIFE moves through me.

9. LIFE is to be lived in love.

10. LIFE is best when I am fully conscious.

11. LIFE is a gift.

Listen

LISTENING IS KEY TO SUCCESS. There are several means by which we should listen. Listen first to the heart. Our heart is the essence of who we are. If something transpires in the environment and we have uncomfortable feelings, then take that feeling into account.

And when we sit and listen, what does our intuition—our third eye, our sixth sense—tell us? Our intuition is direct, and it will never lead us wrong. With consistent meditative practice we will be able to distinguish between the voice of the Higher Self and the voice of the ego, which is fear based and limiting.

Not only do we listen to our heart and our intuition, but we also must listen to others. Yet, in listening to others, we must carefully consider who is giving the message. Are they friends that have proven to always share their thoughts from a neutral, clear perspective, or are their words tainted? Are they what we consider friends who are tuned in or should we tune them out? Do we think it best to go to an expert? And even then, should we get the opinions of several experts before we make our final decision? Whatever the case may be, we must continue to listen for the Word.

POWER STATEMENTS

1. I LISTEN to truth, and success comes to me.

2. I LISTEN to my heart, then I know truth.

3. I LISTEN to my body as well as my heart.

4. I LISTEN to what others are saying
   and what they are not saying.

5. I LISTEN to those who know more than I.

6. I LISTEN to my intimate companions.

7. I LISTEN to the Divine during
   my meditation.

8. I LISTEN to the Divine, and
   wisdom comes forth.

9. I LISTEN to my intuition,
   then I know my path.

10. I LISTEN, then I obey.

11. I LISTEN.

Love

GO THROUGH MUSICAL HISTORY and see how many songs have been written about love. Clearly, it is something that we all want, whether it is romance, friendship, or family love. How do we find it? How do we sustain it? The art of loving, like anything else, is something that has to be cultivated.

Let us start by disciplining the self to surrender to love every moment of the day, whether alone, with others, at work, or at home. Whatever is happening, find the love. Of course, it is challenging to see and feel love in the midst of destruction or death; yet love is present there, too.

When my mother died I must admit that I had trouble experiencing love; I was devastated. Yet, when I processed my mother's death a few weeks after her burial, I realized my beloved mother did not suffer or experience undue pain, considering that she died two weeks after having received a diagnosis of cancer. I had rediscovered love, even after my dear mother's death.

We are all on the planet because something allows us to be; let's call it Love. Consciously, decide to be in love all day. Surrender to the concept that life is a flow of love; it simply needs our participation.

POWER STATEMENTS

1.   LOVE is for all.

2.   LOVE lets me be at peace with
     success and tragedy alike.

3.   LOVE comes when I surrender
     to that which simply is.

4.   LOVE is given to me on every breath.

5.   LOVE lets me live.

6.   LOVE doesn't stop giving.

7.   LOVE allows me to receive, give,
     and expect nothing in return.

8.   LOVE makes everybody feel good.

9.   LOVE is love when the other one feels it.

10. LOVE is.

11. LOVE.

Marriage

MARRIAGE IS A PHENOMENON that differs among cultures. In some cultures, partners choose each other, while in others it is sometimes arranged. Whether chosen or arranged, it is an institution that works best when the partners have worked on their spiritual, mental, and emotional selves to the degree that sacrifice, tolerance, patience, forgiveness, and compassion are always operative. If this is not the case, then the partners in the relationship should revisit the concept of marriage.

POWER STATEMENTS

1. MARRIAGE can be arranged, or partners can freely choose each other.

2. MARRIAGE sometimes brings challenges for two individuals to communicate and negotiate so that life can be lived in harmony.

3. MARRIAGE is helped through sacrifice, patience, and tolerance while maintaining compassion for self and mate.

4. MARRIAGE should be discussed
   to assist in personal/relational/
   financial goals being reached.

5. MARRIAGE is a vow to love the
   relationship more than my ego.

6. MARRIAGE can be at its best when
   I date and learn the other.

7. MARRIAGE is a union, a mergence, an
   amalgam that often takes time.

8. MARRIAGE is best when the needs
   of the individuals are also met.

9. MARRIAGE is a journey of
   the involved souls.

10. MARRIAGE is the individuals working
    together to become one.

11. MARRIAGE is a contract made on
    Earth to live a heavenly life.

Masculine Principle

THERE IS THE DIVINE, which has differentiated itself into two operating forces: the Masculine Principle and the Feminine Principle. They are polarities of consciousness; neither is better than the other, simply different.

The Masculine Principle is akin to the sun. It is the light that shines in all situations. It is direction. It is stability. It is dependability. The Masculine Principle plants the seeds for growth.

POWER STATEMENTS

1. MASCULINE PRINCIPLE is embodied in both man and woman.

2. MASCULINE PRINCIPLE is part of the Divine.

3. MASCULINE PRINCIPLE is steady and consistent like the sun.

4. MASCULINE PRINCIPLE is clarity of mind like the light of day.

5. MASCULINE PRINCIPLE is a protective shield like Father Sky.

6. MASCULINE PRINCIPLE seeds ideas and dreams that become the future.

7. MASCULINE PRINCIPLE is the catalyst for growth.

8. MASCULINE PRINCIPLE within individuals is straightforward and rational in being.

9. MASCULINE PRINCIPLE within individuals is tangible, concrete, and structured.

10. MASCULINE PRINCIPLE is solid and grounded.

11. MASCULINE PRINCIPLE works in collaboration with Feminine Principle to create balance.

Mastery

IT IS IN STRIVING to always do our best that we develop mastery. In mastering a craft or a practice, we are actually mastering the self as we discipline ourselves to do the work. The master has discipline, and as we develop that discipline, we become the masters.

POWER STATEMENTS

1. MASTERY requires discipline.

2. MASTERY is being focused, dedicated, and consistent.

3. MASTERY requires time and conscientious work.

4. MASTERY comes through daily practice.

5. MASTERY is surrendering into excellence.

6. MASTERY is turning my innate talents into admirable skills.

7. MASTERY directs me to serve others with my developed skills.

8. MASTERY comes from learning from other masters.

9. MASTERY means being one of the best.

10. MASTERY is revered when humility accompanies.

11. MASTERY can be achieved.

Meditate

HOW UPLIFTING to start or end our day by bringing our individual biorhythm into harmony with the Divine, the universal biorhythm. When we consistently designate time and space to meditative practice, we receive messages from the Divine. In practicing meditation, we cleanse our mind of undue doubts and insecurities. What a blessing to calm the being so that we experience peace and simultaneously develop our intuition to be at the right place at the right time.

We meditate because we love coming into harmony with the self, other selves, and the universal Divine. Now is the time.

POWER STATEMENTS

1. I MEDITATE to cleanse my unconscious of fear, doubt, and insecurity.

2. I MEDITATE to still my restless mind.

3. I MEDITATE as a healing process to be free of thought and desire.

4. I MEDITATE to create clarity of mind.

5. I MEDITATE, and I am divinely guided.

6. I MEDITATE, and eventually I come to Peace.

7. I MEDITATE in the morning to create an ease in the flow of my day-to-day activities.

8. I MEDITATE in the evening to further cleanse my subconscious mind.

9. I MEDITATE to see the unseen and hear the unspoken.

10. I MEDITATE to know the unknown.

11. I MEDITATE to raise my awareness.

Meditation to

CLEANSE
THE SUBCONSCIOUS MIND

SIDDHA: *This meditation activates communication as the thumb touches the Mercury finger, the finger of communication. Consequently, this meditation cleanses the subconscious mind as repressed negative ideas and debilitating images are released, making your waking mind clearer. This meditation also helps prevent nightmares.*

———————○———————

Sit on the floor in easy pose, where your legs are crossed. This posture stills the energy of the lower centers of consciousness and allows us to more easily activate the higher centers of consciousness. You may also simply sit in a chair with your feet flat on the ground. Your spine should be straight and your neck an extension of your spine.

Raise your arms up into surrender pose so that the upper arms are parallel to the ground while the forearms are perpendicular to the upper arms, palms facing outward. Bend the thumb of each hand to where it touches the base of the pinky finger, the Mercury mound. Breathe long and deep for 11 minutes as you focus on the tip of the nose.

Mind

WHERE DOES THE MIND live within us? While we may not fully understand where in the being it resides, its power cannot be denied. It is the mind that is responsible for all our successes and failures. Our mind can lead us astray, cause us to do foolish things, become irrational, and even be destructive.

Yet, when the mind is properly focused, it can create things so incredible that we have to call them miracles. Use meditative practice to bring it under the guidance of a Higher Consciousness. Then your mind will serve your higher good.

POWER STATEMENTS

1. My MIND is faster than the speed of light.

2. My MIND is empowered when the subconscious is cleansed.

3. My MIND must be directed and focused.

4. My MIND is given to me to benefit my life.

5. My MIND can create health, wealth, and happiness.

6. My MIND can bring forth infinite possibilities.

7. My MIND has a conscious relationship with the Divine when I consistently meditate.

8. My MIND, when merged in the Divine, is at one with Divine intelligence.

9. My MIND becomes calm when I meditate.

10. My MIND is my friend.

11. My MIND is mine.

Money

MONEY IS A COMMODITY that represents value. When we, as individuals, begin to value ourselves, money, which signifies value, will flow. Perhaps there have been times when our family, friends, coworkers, or associates devalued or shamed us. Indeed, that is why we must delve into deep-seated, repressed psychic material to see what may be lurking within the depths, so that we can eradicate it and thrive. Who wants to merely survive? Allow ourselves to work on the mental, emotional, and spiritual aspects of our being to heighten our sense of self. Our influx of money will be proportionate to our resolve that we are worthy.

POWER STATEMENTS

1.   MONEY is paper, so I will read and give attention to all paper in my house.

2.   MONEY comes through my efforts, my value of self, and my creativity.

3.   MONEY comes when I discipline myself and believe I deserve it.

4.   MONEY is to be made, saved, and invested.

5.   MONEY is part of life.

6.   MONEY is key to living well.

7.   MONEY gives me options.

8.   MONEY is a creation.

9.   MONEY can be created.

10. MONEY is freely given to me.

11. MONEY comes to me.

Mother

THERE IS THE MOTHER and there is the father; both are important. Praise be to the mother, whether she is biological, adopted, grandmother, or stepmother. It is her words and actions that empower us to know that we are good. When a mother cares for us, it is imparted to us that we are worthy of care. The "good enough" mother provides caring and compassion.

POWER STATEMENTS

1.   MOTHER I may see as a goddess,
     but she is a human.

2.   MOTHER can smother or give
     me freedom to safely roam.

3.   MOTHER who has fear and
     insecurity shapes my sensitivity
     to others in the world.

4.   MOTHER sets an example of
     caring and compassion.

5.   MOTHER impacts my ability
     to love myself.

6.   MOTHER who sacrifices lets me
     know I am worthy of love.

7.   MOTHER transmits love
     through her touch.

8.   MOTHER gives me confidence
     when she believes in me.

9.   MOTHER does her best; the latter
     part of life, I must do the rest.

10. MOTHER can be a source of safety.

11. MOTHER nurtures my life.

Motivation

WHERE DO WE FIND the motivation to do anything? There is always something to do: wash the dishes, pay the bills, get the car serviced, and so on. The real chore is how to get and stay motivated. Motivation can come about when we mentally inspire ourselves, energize our bodies (exercise, drink tea, etc.) and do our spiritual work to activate the spirit. Get going.

POWER STATEMENTS

1. MOTIVATION is necessary to create the life I want.

2. MOTIVATION conquers the malaise of feeling sorry for myself.

3. MOTIVATION compels me to look at my weaknesses, fears, and laziness, so that I can reach my goal.

4. MOTIVATION sometimes wanes, but I keep focused on my goal.

5. MOTIVATION is what I need to make progress toward reaching my goals.

6. MOTIVATION helps me keep what I have already attained in life.

7. MOTIVATION rubs off on me when I am around people who are mentally focused and physically activated.

8. MOTIVATION can come from others, but I must sustain it.

9. MOTIVATION tells me to get up and get going.

10. MOTIVATION takes me over the finish line.

11. MOTIVATION tells me to do what must be done.

New

EVERY SECOND of the day is new. This is a living, moving universe. Allow us not to become rigid. Allow us to embrace the ever-present concept that life is forever new by staying open and ready for that which comes into our energy field.

POWER STATEMENTS

1. NEW is forever presenting itself in this Age of Aquarius, the age of knowing.

2. NEW can be hard to accept.

3. NEW sometimes scares me.

4. NEW inspires me to look at the way I used to do things.

5. NEW encourages me to be open to change.

6. NEW can shake me out of a rut.

7. NEW replaces the old to keep things fresh.

8. NEW should be tested to see if it improves my life; sometimes it does not.

9. NEW, sometimes, must be embraced to keep up with the times.

10. NEW is every day; I have another chance.

11. NEW is now.

Opportunity

OPPORTUNITY PRESENTS ITSELF every day. An opportunity is a moment within life: an occasion to create, a chance to connect with friends, and a time to study and learn. It could also be a moment where, if we drank from its cup, it could disrupt our possibility to excel in life. We must accustom ourselves to "listen into the space" and hear what is being asked of us. What do we do with the opportunity presented?

POWER STATEMENTS

1. OPPORTUNITY is an invitation
    from the Divine.

2. OPPORTUNITY presents itself all the time.

3. OPPORTUNITY is sent to me to stir my
    thoughts, feelings, and consciousness.

4. OPPORTUNITY tells me I have been chosen.

5. OPPORTUNITY says think about
    how my life will be affected.

6. OPPORTUNITY can be a moment for
    me to relax and have fun.

7. OPPORTUNITY can be a chance
    to use my talents and skills.

8. OPPORTUNITY presents itself through
    ideas, people, and possibilities.

9. OPPORTUNITY allows me to find
    those people who will help me on
    my journey, if I need assistance.

10. OPPORTUNITY is here to acknowledge
    others and discover why we are
    together in this time and space.

11. OPPORTUNITY can prosper my life.

Organization

ORGANIZATION IS LINKED to prosperity. When we put everything in its place and deal with bills as they come, situations as they arise, every piece of paper that passes through our house, we are signaling to the universe that we can handle matter; consequently, the universe will give us more. There is no vacuum in the Divine's creation, so when we place things where they belong and handle that which is given to us, the universe dishes out more for us to handle.

Once there was a gentleman who came to me in my private practice who was bored, with no vision of what he wanted to do. The assignment I gave him was to organize everything in his small apartment, which culminated in him finding sheet music that reminded him he had a BA in Voice from a reputable college. Subsequently, he resumed taking singing classes. Several weeks later he went to an audition and became the understudy to the lead in a long-running Broadway production. Start organizing; clarity, purpose, and prosperity will follow.

POWER STATEMENTS

1. ORGANIZATION is the *O* of God.

2. ORGANIZATION is bringing order
    to my life.

3. ORGANIZATION often requires
    assistance from others.

4. ORGANIZATION brings peace.

5. ORGANIZATION prepares me for
    upcoming opportunity.

6. ORGANIZATION is the mandate of those
    who, eventually, want to be in charge.

7. ORGANIZATION is the process where
    I begin to take charge of my life.

8. ORGANIZATION creates play time.

9. ORGANIZATION helps restore balance
    when the unexpected shows up.

10. ORGANIZATION is something
    I am deepening into.

11. ORGANIZATION is integral to success
    and allows me to maintain it.

Pain

PAIN IS MULTIDIMENSIONAL. There are those who experience physical pain from a wound or a debilitating disease, while others may experience emotional pain from anguished mentality or overriding fear to such an extent that panic attacks occur. Then, too, spiritual pain that arises when we cannot find contentment is just as disconcerting. Regardless of whether it is spiritual, physical, mental, or emotional pain, it hurts. To deepen into our pain is a means of understanding its cause.

POWER STATEMENTS

1.   PAIN hurts, whether it is physical, mental, emotional, or spiritual.

2.   PAIN is talking loud and clear.

3.   PAIN felt is pain recognized.

4.   PAIN is not what I want to feel.

5.   PAIN reminds me to be conscious, so I can avoid pain in the future.

6.   PAIN directs me to ask the question, "What can I do?"

7.   PAIN inspires me to engage in a conversation to discover its cause.

8.   PAIN forces me to change my way of being in the world so that I can be pain-free.

9.   PAIN is a catalyst for transformation.

10. PAIN moves me to change and expand.

11. PAIN is asking for my attention.

Patience

PATIENCE IS THE ATTRIBUTE where we consciously surrender to the reality that things are moving around us. We do what we do, and the things of the world do what they do. Sometimes we can speed up the movement of things of the world and other times we cannot. One who is patient is relaxed and comfortable with delay. The patient individual knows that things happen and are always happening in Divine time.

POWER STATEMENTS

1.   PATIENCE is waiting to receive the knowledge I need to succeed.

2.   PATIENCE is integral to overcoming obstacles as I await the solution.

3.   PATIENCE allows me to be carefree and comfortable with delay.

4.   PATIENCE requires me to let go of expectations and desires.

5.   PATIENCE knows that everything happens in Divine time.

6.   PATIENCE is revealed as I focus on whatever is presently happening or I am doing.

7.   PATIENCE rises as I merge into the now.

8.   PATIENCE is relaxing into the process and not focusing on the outcome.

9.   PATIENCE is deepening me into relaxation, so I become stress-free.

10.   PATIENCE is embodied in the peace that accompanies me as I walk my personal journey.

11.   PATIENCE lives when I quiet my mind.

Meditation for
HEALING

SIDDHA: *This meditation is all about changing the color of our auras to impact our physical well-being. The aura is our attractive force; it brings things and situations to us. The color yellow is associated with physical health and an inspired, alive being. If you are dealing with a symptom in your body, begin to picture this radiant yellow light completely surrounding you as you impact your health and well-being. If you can change the color of your aura, you can shift your physical body as well as your environment.*

Sit on the floor in easy pose, where your legs are crossed. This posture stills the energy of the lower centers of consciousness and allows us to more easily activate the higher centers of consciousness. You may also simply sit in a chair with your feet flat on the floor to ground yourself. Your spine should be straight and your neck an extension of your spine. Hands should be in Gyan Mudra (see page 33) as they rest on the thighs with the palms up or down. Calm yourself as you become conscious of the breath. Breathe long and deep through your nose as you begin to tune in to the auric energy surrounding your body. Sit quietly as you imagine a bright yellow radiant light around you. See yourself encased in this light 8 feet in all directions. Begin practicing this meditation for 3 minutes at a time and build up to 11 minutes a day. When you see the light surrounding your physical body, bask in it.

People

YES, PEOPLE ARE ON THE PLANET. And it looks like we have to live with them. They are everywhere: at home, at work, in the streets, on television, at school, even on vacation. Then they multiply, talk, walk, and sometimes invade our space. What is one to do?

But, they also can bless us. Begin to see the living Divine within them all, even though they themselves may not be in touch with this vital force. Serve them and gracefully be with them.

Sometimes they can induce harm, whether intentional or unintentional. They have different perspectives from us. They can unnecessarily act out unresolved issues and project their pain onto us through inappropriate communication. Work with them, play with them, and know that they are here to stay.

POWER STATEMENTS

1. PEOPLE live alongside me.

2. PEOPLE are my mother, father, family, children, friends, acquaintances, and cohorts.

3. PEOPLE often have different perspectives from me.

4. PEOPLE sometimes disappoint me.

5. PEOPLE sometimes have to be redirected.

6. PEOPLE can deter or stimulate my personal growth.

7. PEOPLE can be my teachers.

8. PEOPLE do things that deepen me into the reality that I must remain conscious throughout the day.

9. PEOPLE show me the necessity of love.

10. PEOPLE irritate me when I lose awareness of their divinity within.

11. PEOPLE embody the Divine, just like me.

Play

LIFE WITHOUT PLAY is boring. As we get older we think play is just for children. But, just as we instruct children that they can't play all the time and also must do chores or work, so it is with adults that we must find balance and remind ourselves that we can't work all the time. We must also play.

POWER STATEMENTS

1. PLAY lifts my spirit.

2. PLAY is letting go and flowing in freedom.

3. PLAY is being carefree.

4. PLAY makes me feel childlike.

5. PLAY is essential to my happiness.

6. PLAY keeps me in balance.

7. PLAY is the creativity in my work.

8. PLAYTIME is necessary.

9. PLAYTIME is something I must set aside regularly.

10. PLAY is fun.

11. PLAYTIME is now.

Power

DO WE FEEL the power within? Can we own it? Assuredly, we want to gracefully and humbly live in our power. Each of us is a powerhouse, but we also must recognize the power within others. As Lord Acton wrote, "All power corrupts, and absolute power corrupts absolutely." However, the Pocket Guru focuses us on the idea that when the power within merges with the power without—the Divine—we become powerful. It is then that we must become responsible and use our power to uplift ourselves and others.

POWER STATEMENTS

1. POWER is within me, and
   power is within you.

2. POWER abused is an act of hubris.

3. POWER is knowing and relating
   consciously to the Divine within.

4. POWER can be mental, physical,
   emotional, or spiritual.

5. POWER directed in the mental
   realm is creativity.

6. POWER directed in the physical
   realm is strength.

7. POWER directed in the emotional
   realm is passion.

8. POWER directed in the spiritual
   realm can create miracles.

9. POWER used correctly empowers
   others as well as myself.

10. POWER is Divine.

11. POWER is mine to claim.

Problems

ALLOW US TO REFRAME our thinking. Rather than processing something as a problem, begin to proclaim it as merely a moment in time and space to use our intelligence, resources, and depth. The sun does not always shine, and so it is within our own personal lives that we will have moments of darkness. When we understand that darkness is part of life, we will see troubling moments simply as an invitation to sit in the light of consciousness. Let us pick up our lantern and proceed into the dark, ready to embrace the opportunity to use our wisdom.

POWER STATEMENTS

1. PROBLEMS are opportunities
    to employ my wisdom.

2. PROBLEMS come from the
    Divine to test my trust.

3. PROBLEMS are hiccups that
    interrupt my peace.

4. PROBLEMS are merely moments
    in time and space.

5. PROBLEMS stimulate me
    to be resourceful.

6. PROBLEMS activate my common
    sense as well as my sixth sense.

7. PROBLEMS can be reframed.

8. PROBLEMS are a matter of perception.

9. PROBLEMS dissolve as faith arrives.

10. PROBLEMS can be resolved.

11. PROBLEMS require my focus and will.

Purpose

EVERYONE WANTS TO KNOW their purpose on this Earth. The question resounds loudly: "What am I to do while I am here?" Our purpose during this existence is ultimately to come into the realization that we are simply consciousness. When we live in purpose, the Divine is working through us to bless humanity in our unique way. We search; we try things until we find our purpose. Finding purpose is surrendering to the call of our soul.

POWER STATEMENTS

1. PURPOSE offers a clear answer to
   what I should do with my life.

2. PURPOSE leads to goodwill
   toward myself and others.

3. PURPOSE can be demanding,
   but I do not give up.

4. PURPOSE makes me feel engaged.

5. PURPOSE uses my unique
   qualities and talents.

6. PURPOSE allows me to brush aside
   the disapproval of others.

7. PURPOSE has been recognized; I feel it.

8. PURPOSE resounds in hearing
   the call of my soul.

9. PURPOSE is found as I move in trust.

10. PURPOSE makes me feel
    energized and alive.

11. PURPOSE gives meaning to my life.

Regret

I WAS SITTING at my mother's deathbed, minutes before she died. Although my mother could understand everything I was saying, she could no longer speak. The only way she could respond was to nod her head. I was soothing my mother and giving thanks for all she had done for me. During this very intimate moment, I took a chance to ask my mother if she had any regrets. Surprisingly, she nodded her head. I was overcome with such sadness that whatever my mother had or had not done during her life had caused her regret. My mother had given me one last lesson before she entered the great unknown: go for your dreams, make conscious decisions, and do what you must, so that you will never have regrets.

POWER STATEMENTS

1. REGRET is here.

2. REGRET lingers.

3. REGRET reminds me that I am unfulfilled.

4. REGRET says, "I think I made a mistake."

5. REGRET is trying to deny me
    a renewed life.

6. REGRET challenges me to
    live once again fully.

7. REGRET cannot undo what has been done.

8. REGRET dissolves, and I remember
    that I am still breathing.

9. REGRET can be reversed, and I can find joy.

10. REGRET leaves as I focus on possibility.

11. REGRET is gone.

Relationships

ALL OF LIFE is built on relationships: with self, the Divine, and others. It is when we bring the self in alignment with the Divine that our relationships will be consciously driven. Of course, meditative practice induces this.

Relationships prosper when we have an awareness of self and others, even though, at times, they may be challenging. When they go awry, it is time to question why we were triggered. Perhaps it enlightens us to understand that the decision one ultimately makes depends on a host of complex factors: culture, family upbringing, gender, age, sexual orientation, ethnicity. Allow us to consciously relate to self and others. As beings we live with ourselves, with others, and with the Divine. Yet, from a Higher Consciousness perspective, it would be commendable if we learn to live for ourselves, for others, and for the Divine. These relationships would then be rooted in a principle that would create a world where we live in Divine Love.

POWER STATEMENTS

1. RELATIONSHIPS can be hard.

2. RELATIONSHIPS reflect who
    I am and how I am.

3. RELATIONSHIPS teach me a lot about myself.

4. RELATIONSHIPS with others are impacted
    by my relationship with myself.

5. RELATIONSHIPS with others bring
    up my unresolved issues.

6. RELATIONSHIPS are like ships that relay
    messages back and forth—they can move
    forward only when all parties involved
    keep the lines of communication open.

7. RELATIONSHIPS with others that are
    personally fulfilling make me feel alive.

8. RELATIONSHIPS with others
    stimulate and activate me.

9. RELATIONSHIPS require time and patience.

10. RELATIONSHIPS are harmonious
    when I deal with others from
    their level of consciousness.

11. RELATIONSHIPS with others thrive when I
    engage in heart-to-heart communication.

Relaxation

TO BE RELAXED as we engage in all our endeavors is a worthy goal. How can we do that? First of all, wherever we are, regardless of the task (speaking up for yourself, looking through the bills, etc.) relax into it. Ways of relaxing among individuals differ. Taking a bath? Going for a short stroll? Doing Tai Chi? Whatever induces that peace of mind and freedom from worry, do it.

POWER STATEMENTS

1. RELAXATION is the art of letting go.

2. RELAXATION takes away my
    worry, tension, and stress.

3. RELAXATION helps get me through the day.

4. RELAXATION needs to occur every day.

5. RELAXATION can be with friends, family,
    or coworkers, and even when I'm alone.

6. RELAXATION can be created by
    taking time off, being with nature,
    or reading for pleasure.

7. RELAXATION comes when I give
    myself permission to relax.

8. RELAXATION comes when my mind
    is in harmony with my spirit.

9. RELAXATION heals the body
    and soothes the mind.

10. RELAXATION helps me rejuvenate.

11. RELAXATION makes me serene.

Reputation

BEING TRUSTWORTHY, serviceable, and reliable will certainly give us a flattering reputation. Our reputation will go places we will never go nor have we ever been. It is an energy force that travels and can bring fortune or infamy. Decide to be reputable.

POWER STATEMENTS

1. My REPUTATION precedes me as others talk about me without me knowing.

2. My REPUTATION will go places that I have never been.

3. My REPUTATION garners me respect because I treat others with respect.

4. My REPUTATION is good because my work ethic is excellent.

5. My REPUTATION is good because I keep my word.

6. My REPUTATION is good because I am punctual.

7. My REPUTATION is good because I am trustworthy.

8. My REPUTATION is good, and that brings me referrals for my work.

9. My REPUTATION is good, and therefore my time is in demand.

10. My REPUTATION increases my personal value.

11. My REPUTATION is my best public relation.

Meditation to
ENHANCE INTUITION

SIDDHA: *The first part of the meditation will raise the etheric energy of the being into the higher centers of consciousness, from the heart chakra to the third eye. It will uplift the psyche as you begin to feel light in spirit. The second part of the meditation will develop your intuition. You will begin to know the unknown and see the unseen.*

PART ONE: Sit on the floor in easy pose, where your legs are crossed. This posture stills the energy of the lower centers of consciousness and allows us to more easily activate the higher centers of consciousness. You may also simply sit in a chair with your feet flat on the floor to ground yourself. Your spine should be straight and your neck an extension of your spine. Interlace the fingers of your right hand with the fingers of the left hand. Palms at the level of the heart chakra should be facing down, forearms parallel to the ground. As you inhale, raise the arms with the hands interlaced up to the third eye; on the exhale, lower the arms, hands still interlaced back down to the level of the heart chakra. This is a rather fast-paced rhythm. Inhale, exhale, inhale, exhale. Keep this up for 3 minutes.

PART TWO: Continue sitting in your same posture. Now position your hands in Gyan Mudra (see page 33) as they rest on the thighs with palms up or down. The focus will be at your third eye at the root of your nose, between the two eyebrows. Eyes should be one-tenth open. Begin to chant *Laaaaaa*. Focus the sound at the third eye. Feel its resonance at the third eye. When you run out of breath, inhale again and begin chanting the sound again. You can practice chanting this sound up to 11 minutes.

Resentment

RESENTMENT IS A FEELING which results from the ideation that someone has transgressed against us. It is the feeling that someone, in some way, has done something or failed to do something that we were expecting. What to do? It now sits inside of us and separates us from others. It can also create a symptom in our body. Resentment is a feeling that can mar our lives if we continue to harbor it. We have to instead find a way to let it go. Allow the following 11 statements to begin the path of healing.

POWER STATEMENTS

1. RESENTMENT comes from feeling that I have been disrespected.

2. RESENTMENT is the unresolved hurt that someone did not meet my expectation.

3. RESENTMENT is my attempt to protect myself from further disrespect, but I still hurt.

4.   RESENTMENT inhibits me
from communicating with
those who hurt me.

5.   RESENTMENT can cause me to
isolate and withdraw.

6.   RESENTMENT festers when
I do not let it go.

7.   RESENTMENT must be released so
that my hurt will not contaminate
my future relationships.

8.   RESENTMENT can be diminished
in my attempt to effectively
communicate my hurt.

9.   RESENTMENT tells me that I
must accept others as they are,
not as I wish them to be.

10.   RESENTMENT says, "I must forgive
myself for being blindsided."

11.   RESENTMENT, I let go.

Resilience

WHO HAS NOT HAD SETBACKS? A setback is simply a setup to test our determination. Keep your eye on the prize, take a deep breath, brush yourself off, and get back on the track of life.

POWER STATEMENTS

1. RESILIENCE is bouncing back no matter what has happened.

2. RESILIENCE tells me that I can overcome obstacles.

3. RESILIENCE is knowing that this is simply life's test of my will.

4. RESILIENCE acknowledges my self-pity but tells me that it does not serve me.

5. RESILIENCE overcomes sorrow and regret.

6. RESILIENCE tells me to reassess and try again.

7. RESILIENCE is what allows me to get back up.

8. RESILIENCE activates my willpower.

9. RESILIENCE reminds me that I must push forward.

10. RESILIENCE focuses on completion, victory, and success.

11. RESILIENCE knows no defeat; I persevere.

Resistance

RESISTANCE HAS A PURPOSE. What is our resistance trying to communicate to us? Why is it there? Listen. Do not fight your resistance. Be with it as you allow it to guide you from your greatest fear to your highest good. For whatever reason, you are not ready to make that move.

POWER STATEMENTS

1. RESISTANCE does exist.

2. RESISTANCE is to be processed;
    it is there for a reason.

3. RESISTANCE says, "I'm not ready to move."

4. RESISTANCE is sometimes
    present to protect us.

5. RESISTANCE gives me a respite
    to process my next move.

6. RESISTANCE indicates some
    perceived anxiety.

7. RESISTANCE exists because I
    have some concerns.

8. RESISTANCE can get in the way of
    change and a more gratifying life.

9. RESISTANCE can be resolved.

10. RESISTANCE can leave and allow me to
    become clear as to what I should do.

11. RESISTANCE asks that I resolve my
    mental and emotional conflict.

Responsibility

RESPONSIBILITY IS KEY to being an adult. Imagine buying a house. The house does not take care of itself. And so it is with our personal lives. We are responsible for the upkeep of ourselves and our affairs. We have to maintain our mental, emotional, and physical health, pay our bills, maintain our relationships, and figure out how to keep moving forward. And if we cannot do it alone, then it is our responsibility to get others to help us get it done.

POWER STATEMENTS

1.   RESPONSIBILITY means learning what I need to do to be successful.

2.   RESPONSIBILITY means taking care of my mental, emotional, spiritual, and physical health.

3.   RESPONSIBILITY cannot be diverted by blaming others for mishaps that have occurred in my life.

4. RESPONSIBILITY causes me to work through my uncomfortable feelings when they arise.

5. RESPONSIBILITY turns my weaknesses into strengths.

6. RESPONSIBILITY means being accountable.

7. RESPONSIBILITY is pursuing my passions and creating my own happiness.

8. RESPONSIBILITY means doing the necessary work.

9. RESPONSIBILITY is taking care of my business affairs.

10. RESPONSIBILITY asks that I have a loving relationship with order.

11. RESPONSIBILITY is the maintenance required to keep my life on track.

Sadness

NOBODY WANTS TO BE SAD; yet if we encounter this uncomfortable feeling, we should not pathologize it. If a pet dies, of course we will be sad. If we get some unsettling news about a friend's misfortune, of course we will be sad. So, sadness in itself is not bad. It is a genuine feeling that has been aroused as something has occurred. Sad is not bad; it just is. We must feel our sadness and work through it. Cry, talk about it, listen to the blues to honor and alleviate sadness. Let sadness live so that it can eventually die. Deny it, and it will overtake us. Feel it, deal with it, and you we will be able to heal it.

POWER STATEMENTS

1. SADNESS is a feeling that is uncomfortable to feel.

2. SADNESS is asking me to sit with my pain.

3. SADNESS alerts me to work through my frustration when things have not turned out the way that I wanted.

4. SADNESS, I feel, when my mind becomes quiet.

5. SADNESS just is.

6. SADNESS is now but not forever.

7. SADNESS is here. Peace is possible.

8. SADNESS can go away.

9. SADNESS fades as hope surfaces.

10. SADNESS was mine.

11. SADNESS, I let go.

Self-Esteem

FINDING SELF-ESTEEM is the journey of the soul. Oh, to embrace bravado so that one's highest potential is constellated! To live fearlessly so that wonder is the experience! To speak truth effectively so that all marvel while simultaneously being elevated in consciousness! To surrender to courage so that meaning in life is felt! To be or not to be is never the question; it is, more so, who we are is who we must be.

POWER STATEMENTS

1.   My SELF-ESTEEM is high as I
     unite with my Higher Self.

2.   My SELF-ESTEEM is high as
     I trust my intuition.

3.   My SELF-ESTEEM is high as I
     share myself with others.

4.   My SELF-ESTEEM is high as I
     tell others how I feel.

5.   My SELF-ESTEEM is high as I listen with
     neutrality to what others tell me.

6.   My SELF-ESTEEM is high as I relax and
     let others admire and adore me.

7.   My SELF-ESTEEM is high as I relax
     and let another intimately love me.

8.   My SELF-ESTEEM is high as I declare,
     "I have the right to be happy."

9.   My SELF-ESTEEM is high as I
     follow the desires of my heart.

10. My SELF-ESTEEM is high as I strive
     to reach my highest potential.

11. My SELF-ESTEEM is high.

Sex

WHAT CONSTITUTES PLEASURE and satisfaction in sex is personal. It should always be between consenting adults. Sex is not to be debased—it is a beautiful connection that should be fulfilling for all involved. Play.

POWER STATEMENTS

1. SEX can bring me into ecstasy.

2. SEX can drain me when I am not mentally, emotionally, or physically stimulated.

3. SEX is heightened with passion.

4. SEX says, "I am willing to please and be pleased."

5. SEX encourages me to please my partner.

6. SEX pleases my wildest imaginations.

7. SEX stimulates creativity.

8. SEX is pleasurable, and I take pleasure in it.

9. SEX can be fun.

10. SEX is best when my mind is stimulated, my heart is moved, and my loins are longing.

11. SEX is playful.

209

Shame

SHAME IS A debilitating feeling. It can pull us into the depths of despair and lead us to self-destructive behaviors. Shame can darken our pathway and keep us from finding love, financial security, and happiness. Shame must be eradicated for us to appreciate and enjoy life.

POWER STATEMENTS

1. SHAME is that feeling that makes
   me feel not good enough.

2. SHAME will not let my light shine bright.

3. SHAME makes me feel invisible.

4. SHAME destroys my appreciation of self.

5. SHAME lives if I shame another or
   allow myself to be shamed.

6. SHAME can be overcome when
   I disavow disrespect.

7. SHAME is eliminated when I envision
   the moment of disrespect and
   release the frozen hurt that I feel.

8. SHAME leaves when I feel the
   presence of the Divine love.

9. SHAME goes away when I say, "I love
   myself, I trust myself, I will be myself."

10. SHAME gone, I am free to be.

11. SHAME, no more.

Spirituality

TO BE SPIRITUAL is to consciously tune into that spirit within. Do we take time to sit and be with our spirit to see what the spirit wants? And if we do know what the spirit wants, do we consciously go against it as we engage in activities that do not inspire us? Are we living a life that is in harmony with the flow of our spirit?

Spirituality is not the same as being religious. It is simply a recognition that the Divine power that moves through the universe also moves through us. Allow us to start getting cozy with the power within as we deepen into spirituality.

POWER STATEMENTS

1.   SPIRITUALITY is how I honor the Divine
     presence flowing through me.

2.   SPIRITUALITY is being kind,
     truthful, and serviceable.

3.   SPIRITUALITY allows me to surrender
     to the call of my inner being.

4.   SPIRITUALITY is trusting the
     unseen spirit within.

5.   SPIRITUALITY comes when I stop
     my restless mind and simply be.

6.   SPIRITUALITY is when my spirit
     says, "Move," and I move.

7.   SPIRITUALITY allows things to happen
     through me rather than willfully by me.

8.   SPIRITUALITY gives way to spontaneity.

9.   SPIRITUALITY is relishing in the
     creative flow of my spirit.

10. SPIRITUALITY is relaxing in the
     flow of my spirit.

11. SPIRITUALITY is synonymous
     with being authentic.

Meditation to
ATTAIN GOALS

SIDDHA: *This meditation is for deepening your ability to create your own reality. Envision what you want to happen and give it focused energy as you assist in bringing it into existence.*

Sit on the floor in easy pose, where your legs are crossed. This posture stills the energy of the lower centers of consciousness and allows us to more easily activate the higher centers of consciousness. You may also simply sit in a chair with your feet flat on the floor to ground yourself. Your spine should be straight and your neck an extension of your spine. Hands should be in Gyan Mudra (see page 33) as they rest on the thighs with palms up or down.

Focus on your third eye, located at the root of the nose between the eyebrows, and begin to see what you would like to transpire in your life. Is it an important examination that you absolutely must pass? Is it a meeting that you want to go a certain way? Is it a relationship that you would like to develop? If you can see it, it can happen. You may have difficulty seeing the details. You may not be able to see what you would like to transpire. You may see something completely different than what you would like. If you cannot envision what you want, consider the possibility that it may not happen. Do not judge what you see. Practice this meditation for 3 to 11 minutes daily. If you can see it, it can happen. You are a collaborator in the art and science of creating. If the goal, for example, is to bring a long-term relationship into being, this meditation should be done for a minimum of 40 days for the best results.

Strategy

HAVING A CLEAR STRATEGY is vital to attaining success. First, we should define our goals within the arena that we are focusing on. Financial success? Prospering career? Fulfilling relationships? In whatever arena we wish to attain our goal, the key is work. Sometimes we do not know what to do or where to go. Sometimes we may know where we want to be, but we do not know how to get there. Rather than always trying to go and get it, the Pocket Guru additionally presents the strategy of working on ourselves and letting it come to us. Through dedicated meditative practice, we will become at one with ourselves; we will develop such a union with the self that the Divine will find us.

POWER STATEMENTS

1. STRATEGY is envisioning what I want and then planning how to skillfully move forward.

2.   STRATEGY should be used for creating health, wealth, and happiness.

3.   STRATEGY is surrendering to my intuition.

4.   STRATEGY is heightened through my awareness of self, others, and my environment.

5.   STRATEGY comes when I start the day with meditation; the Divine will eventually tell me what I need to know and what to do.

6.   STRATEGY tells me to seek help when I need it.

7.   STRATEGY can be learned from others, but I must maneuver in my own way.

8.   STRATEGY offers clarity about my course of action.

9.   STRATEGY is designed to manifest my vision.

10. STRATEGY says trust the flow of my spirit.

11. STRATEGY is mastering the self and letting the Divine find me.

Stress

STRESS COMES WHEN something happens in the environment and we find it challenging to mentally adjust. The reality is that we become stressed because we are having difficulty accepting simply what is. We can alleviate stress when we witness what is happening around us and then, after everything is said and done, consciously decide to accept what is. Allow our meditative consciousness to actively deal with everything that is presented to us and there will be no stress.

POWER STATEMENTS

1. STRESS tells me I am having
    trouble mentally adjusting.

2. STRESS causes me to doubt my ability
    to overcome challenging moments.

3. STRESS gets my adrenaline going.

4. STRESS reveals the distress
    within my mind.

5. STRESS is just a state of mind.

6. STRESS, express, de-stress.

7. STRESS must leave so that my
    health is not affected.

8. STRESS leaves when I accept what is.

9. STRESS leaves as I listen to the Divine
    and hear, "Relax your nerves."

10. STRESS leaves and peace comes.

11. STRESS is gone.

Struggle

STRUGGLING IS A FRAME OF MIND. Whatever is happening in the environment is happening. To scream and holler and try to make it go away induces discomfort. What is happening simply is. Surrender and move through it, consciously. When we are in the dark tunnel, we have to keep walking to get to the exit where there's light. Relax.

POWER STATEMENTS

1. STRUGGLE is exhausting. I am
    ready for a new frame of mind.

2. STRUGGLE was in my past, but it
    will not be a part of my future.

3. STRUGGLE leaves because my developed
    meditative mind tells me what to do.

4. STRUGGLE ceases as I relax into
    the reality of the moment.

5. STRUGGLE is overcome as I look
    for the good in the moment.

6. STRUGGLE is gone when I surrender and
    allow the universe to move around me.

7. STRUGGLE with others is
    no longer an option.

8. STRUGGLE redirects me: I relax into what
    is happening; it is the Divine flow.

9. STRUGGLE used to be part of my
    process, but now I go with the flow.

10. STRUGGLE leaves and I find peace.

11. STRUGGLE. I am done with it.

Success

SUCCESS STARTS with drive. If we believe in our ability to succeed, then success can, eventually, be ours. But success in what? There are many arenas of success—financial, business, social, mental, personal, relationship, sexual, family, physical, spiritual—and they all require focus. Decide what arena is asking for your attention, then proceed in pursuit of success.

POWER STATEMENTS

1. SUCCESS starts with seeing
    myself as successful.

2. SUCCESS tells me to think, act,
    feel, and talk success.

3. SUCCESS tells me to pay
    attention to the details.

4. SUCCESS means being healthy,
    happy, and financially secure.

5. SUCCESS means different things; I
    must decide what it means for me.

6. SUCCESS says, "Seek advice, mentors,
    and the company of successful people."

7. SUCCESS is enhanced when I attract and
    work with those who support my vision.

8. SUCCESS is achieved through
    determination and discipline.

9. SUCCESS requires perseverance.

10. SUCCESS says, "Capitalize on
    the opportunity."

11. SUCCESS is for me.

Suffer

WHY DO WE SUFFER? We may suffer because we get involved with the wrong people who lead us astray or into situations that will have negative repercussions. We may also suffer because we forget the law of karma, which states that for every action there is an equal and opposite reaction. Lastly, we may suffer because of samskaras, the karma with which we come into the life. To process the samskaras, we takes into consideration the country in which we were born, our gender and family, the perennial challenges and life lessons which confront us.

Suffering can be diminished or avoided entirely when we commit to meditative practice on a daily basis, so that we are always being intuitively guided and protected. Yet, if for whatever reason we have succumbed to suffering, allow the following 11 statements to assist in restoring mental peace.

POWER STATEMENTS

1. I SUFFER; I feel lifeless.

2. I SUFFER because my ego was not fulfilled.

3. I SUFFER because of my expectation.

4. I SUFFER because I thought I
    was in complete control.

5. I SUFFER when I forget life
    is a flow of the Divine.

6. I SUFFER when I wish to be some
    place other than "here."

7. I SUFFER less when I become
    open to possibility.

8. I SUFFER less when I surrender
    to the moment.

9. I SUFFER less when I sing, "Peace be still."

10. I SUFFER less when love
    overtakes my thoughts.

11. I SUFFER not when I realize that the
    Divine is present even in this moment.

Suicide

IT IS VERY UNSETTLING to think that anyone can get to the point where suicidal ideation enters the mind. Suicide does not solve any problem. And from the perspective of the Pocket Guru, it is the worst thing that we can do, as the body will die but the soul will still live, estranged on the planet. For those who did, however, willfully take their lives, the soul left out of one of the ten holes in the body, even though the eternal soul remained locked in the magnetic field of the Earth. No one can see them or hear them; this is commonly referred to as a ghost.

The individual soul must work through a body on planet Earth; it must work out its karma, then go back home to merge with the Universal Soul, the Divine, Pure Consciousness. After death, it has been calculated that the body is a quarter of an ounce lighter; perhaps the difference is the weight of the soul.

POWER STATEMENTS

1. SUICIDE has entered my mind.

2. SUICIDE is not an elevating thought.

3. SUICIDE was a thought passing through my psyche.

4. SUICIDE negates the Divine that gave me life.

5. SUICIDE clings to cowardice and rejects courage.

6. SUICIDE kills the body, but the soul will be left estranged on the planet.

7. SUICIDE is a thought that must be redirected by working through hopelessness and self-hatred to belief in the divinity of the self.

8. SUICIDE is not a viable emotional outlet; I will work through my dark mood to creative expression.

9. SUICIDE will not make me happier; I will deepen into unconditional self-love.

10. SUICIDE will not solve my problems.

11. SUICIDE is not the answer; I will live my life with courage.

Surrender

TO SURRENDER is to give up being positive or negative about a situation. When we are in a state of surrender, we are neutral. And when we are neutral we are at one with the Divine. The Pocket Guru utilizes the term *the Divine*; however, we may refer to it as *Energy, Higher Self, Unlimitedness of Being, the Beyond, the Infinite Creative Consciousness*. It does not matter, as long as we understand that it is this all-encompassing Force to which we are surrendering. In a state of surrender we will have arrived at oneness: I am thou; we are one. In that time and space, the mind, soul, and heart will synchronize as we deepen into possibility.

POWER STATEMENTS

1. SURRENDER is challenged by
    my will, my ego.

2. SURRENDER to the Divine will is a loss
    to my ego, but a victory to my spirit.

3. SURRENDER is a powerful moment
    when my little ego merges with
    the universal ego.

4. SURRENDER becomes easy when I
    let go of my need to control.

5. SURRENDER makes me feel out of control,
    but in reality, I am gaining control.

6. SURRENDER begins when I
    become desireless.

7. SURRENDER is a state of neutrality.

8. SURRENDER ultimately brings
    peace and fulfillment.

9. SURRENDER brings me into harmony.

10. SURRENDER lives with trust.

11. SURRENDER is not giving up; it is
    letting go into the Divine.

Teacher

IN MANY WAYS we come into the world, as John Locke says, with a "tabula rasa," a clean slate. We must learn how to make it in life. The teacher comes when we are ready to learn. When we are willing to be a student, the teacher will appear. We need teachers.

POWER STATEMENTS

1. My TEACHER appears when
   I am ready to learn.

2. My TEACHER is respectful of me.

3. My TEACHER is my mother, father,
   friends, and coworkers.

4. My TEACHER can be life itself as it
   presents its trials and situations.

5. My TEACHER shows me what
   to do and what not to do.

6. My TEACHER shows me what serves
   me and what does not serve me.

7. My TEACHER tests me; I must
   master the lesson.

8. My TEACHER tells me to bow
   to teachings of truth.

9. My TEACHER says, "Job well done."

10. My TEACHER presents the
    teachings, but I must practice.

11. My TEACHER prepares me to
    possibly become the teacher.

Thoughts

WHAT ARE WE THINKING? What have we consciously or unconsciously attracted into our lives? As we look around, we see what has appeared in our life; this is indicative of what we have been thinking.

What we are thinking is one of the important factors that determines what happens in our future. Change our thoughts, and we change the world around us. Create what we want by thinking about what we want. The universe is simply a computer; it prints out what we put in.

POWER STATEMENTS

1. THOUGHTS are in my conscious
mind and thoughts are also in
my subconscious mind.

2. THOUGHTS create feelings and
feelings create desires.

3. THOUGHTS determine my behaviors.

4. THOUGHTS come to me and I consciously
decide upon which thought to focus.

5. THOUGHTS are powerful.

6. THOUGHTS are creative units
in time and space.

7. THOUGHTS communicate to
me that I am worthy.

8. THOUGHTS can lead to success.

9. THOUGHTS can bring prosperous living
(health, wealth, and happiness).

10. THOUGHTS I focus on bring
me what I want.

11. THOUGHTS can create miracles in my life.

Meditation to

BALANCE

THE LEFT AND RIGHT HEMISPHERES
OF THE BRAIN

SIDDHA: *This meditation is a very simple action that brings serenity. It is designed to balance the right and left hemispheres of the brain, so that the analytical and intuitional sides can come into harmony. This meditation is a tool to develop the ability to process situations with a heightened awareness, and, with regular practice, deep insights are offered into the mysteries of life.*

Sit on the floor in easy pose, where your legs are crossed. This posture stills the energy of the lower centers of consciousness and allows us to more easily activate the higher centers of consciousness. You may also simply sit in a chair with both of your feet on the floor. Your spine should be straight and your neck an extension of your spine. Bring your hands up, palms facing the heart center, the middle of the chest, the sternum. Place the back of one hand in the palm of the other, crossing at a 45-degree angle so that the thumbs cross in the middle of the top palm. It does not matter which hand is on top; the crossing of the thumbs is what is integral to the meditation, as this neutralizes the ego.

We are now ready to begin the four-part breath series: (1) Pucker your lips, as if you are sipping liquid through a straw. When the lungs are completely filled with breath, exhale through the same puckered lips. (2) Inhale long and deep through the nose until you have completely filled the lungs to capacity, then exhale the breath completely out through the nose. (3) Now pucker your lips again as you did in the first pranayama (breathing exercise); inhale through the puckered lips, then exhale through the nose. (4) Lastly, inhale through the nose and exhale through the puckered lips. Start by practicing this meditation for 3 minutes and slowly build up to practicing for 11 minutes.

Time

TOO OFTEN we are driven by time: rushing, behind schedule, feeling as if we do not have enough time. The real deal is that everyone has twenty-four hours within the day. And how we use it is completely up to us. Instead of being controlled by time, or even trying to control it, be at one with it. The individual who masters time is always completely immersed in the moment. This is the way to become timeless.

POWER STATEMENTS

1. TIME on planet Earth is the experience of my now.

2. TIME is given to me, today.

3. TIME gone is time gone.

4. TIME given is the Divine's way of saying, "Live."

5. TIME is asking that I recognize an opportunity in the moment.

6. TIME proposes an opportunity to live and love.

7. TIME reminds me to live passionately from my heart.

8. TIME brings fulfillment when I dare to be myself.

9. TIME that is of importance is present time.

10. TIME becomes mine when I live wholeheartedly in the moment.

11. TIME is now.

Today

TODAY WILL NEVER be duplicated. It is unique, unlike any other. See how the day unfolds. Who has come into our lives today? What situations have presented themselves? Accept the ideas, feelings, events, and persons that present themselves to us today. Consciously deal with it all. Be thankful; it is the flow of the Divine.

POWER STATEMENTS

1. TODAY, I acknowledge the
    Omnipresent Divine.

2. TODAY, I consciously embrace
    each moment.

3. TODAY, I surrender to whatever life brings.

4. TODAY, I let go of expectation and
    am completely present in my life!

5. TODAY is here.

6. TODAY, I live.

7. TODAY, I open up to possibility
    and declare, "I am, I am!"

8. TODAY, I see love everywhere.

9. TODAY, I lovingly present
    myself to the world.

10. TODAY is a blessing.

11. TODAY.

Tomorrow

WE PUT ONE FOOT in front of the other with the hope that tomorrow will come. To prepare today for a good tomorrow is a respectable discipline. Let us be conscientious today so that tomorrow we easily ride the wave. In other words, get an education, choose and master a trade, learn from the learned, develop financial wisdom.

The fairy tale of the three little pigs comes to mind. The third little pig worked hard to build his house of brick. He had a good tomorrow when the wolf tried to blow his house down. Prepare today for a good tomorrow.

POWER STATEMENTS

1.   TOMORROW purports to be best
     when I prepare today.

2.   TOMORROW is often riddled with
     challenges because of yesterday.

3.   TOMORROW can be sunny even
     though today was dark.

4.   TOMORROW is the prayer,
     because today I prayed.

5.   TOMORROW can be envisioned today.

6.   TOMORROW gives me hope
     as I envision it today.

7.   TOMORROW is a new day.

8.   TOMORROW can be better than today.

9.   TOMORROW can bring untold blessings.

10. TOMORROW is the hope of today.

11. TOMORROW is not promised; therefore,
     I live passionately today.

Transitions

CAN WE SIT in the reality that the Earth is moving right now? This is not a static universe, so release the concept that things must remain the same. We transition from infancy to toddlerhood, childhood, teenage years, young adulthood, middle age, and, hopefully, old age. We are constantly in motion and transition.

POWER STATEMENTS

1. TRANSITIONS are merely a
    moment in time and space.

2. TRANSITIONS take me from here to there.

3. TRANSITIONS are taking me
    into the unknown.

4. TRANSITIONS are milestones
    on the journey of life.

5. TRANSITIONS are necessary for my growth.

6. TRANSITIONS are challenging
    only when I resist.

7. TRANSITIONS are easy when I
    surrender to the process.

8. TRANSITIONS tell me to enjoy the process.

9. TRANSITIONS say flow in timelessness.

10. TRANSITIONS are the Divine moving me on.

11. I welcome TRANSITIONS.

Trust

FROM THE PERSPECTIVE of the Pocket Guru, it is not love but trust that is the Highest Consciousness. We can love ourselves, but do we trust ourselves? Allow us to do the mental, emotional, and spiritual work so that we can trust our sensations, feelings, and intuition. Love should be at the core of all our endeavors, but trust is the fuel that propels us into action.

POWER STATEMENTS

1. I TRUST that Divine love is always working on my behalf.

2. I TRUST that this life is an opportunity for me to be myself.

3. I TRUST my heart when it tells me how it feels about a person, situation, or incident.

4. I TRUST myself, so then I know who to trust.

5. I TRUST my intuition, so I will not befall a fate.

6. I TRUST that I will overcome any challenges I face.

7. I TRUST that there is a solution to all perceived problems.

8. I TRUST that I will be successful in my endeavors.

9. I TRUST the uncanny flow of my spirit as it leads me to wonderful discovery.

10. I TRUST, therefore I can.

11. I TRUST myself.

◯ Truth

TRUTH IS DEEPLY PENETRATING. How to express your truth?

With others, truth is to be clearly and effectively communicated. When we speak and live our truth, we are real, authentic. Truth be told and lived.

POWER STATEMENTS

1. TRUTH is what is transpiring in my immediate environment; I must consciously deal with it.

2. TRUTH can help resolve conflict.

3. TRUTH can heal those in doubt, confusion, and dismay.

4. TRUTH, when spoken harshly, can be hurtful to others.

5. TRUTH requires me to be discerning as to when and how to say it.

6. TRUTH, which is unsettling, should be processed, not dismissed.

7. TRUTH is sometimes difficult to hear.

8. TRUTH, when spoken, releases my hurt and pain.

9. TRUTH spoken is what will bring me contentment.

10. TRUTH lived is a soulful life.

11. TRUTH is penetrating.

Understanding

UNDERSTANDING IS CENTRAL to a wholesome outlook on whatever is transpiring. This is especially
true for dealing with other people; often we forget
that others do not always think and see the world
as we do. This can be problematic, as we are prone
to emotional hurt when others do or say something
that we are not expecting.

To deeply understand, get quiet and ask the
Divine, "What is going on?" Wait for your answer.
The ability to receive Divine guidance is enhanced
if we establish an ongoing relation with the Divine
through daily meditation. And if perchance our
understanding of what is going on still is not clear,
then go to another that you respect and ask the
Divine to speak to you through them. Once we
understand, then we can proceed with knowing.

POWER STATEMENTS

1. To have an UNDERSTANDING is to
    be armed with knowledge.

2. To have an UNDERSTANDING is to have
    connected with the superconscious
    mind through meditation.

3. To have an UNDERSTANDING of
the coherence within my life
brings me depth.

4. To have an UNDERSTANDING, I
am assisted by experts, friends,
parents, teachers, and mentors.

5. To have an UNDERSTANDING of practical
living skills is vital, for I must survive.

6. To have an UNDERSTANDING is to know
what to do and also what not to do.

7. To have an UNDERSTANDING is the ability to
stand under a person, a situation, as well
as a different outlook to gain perspective.

8. To have an UNDERSTANDING of my
intimate companions, business/
career, and life situation is important,
so I can proceed with acuity.

9. To have an UNDERSTANDING of others'
feelings as well as their way of
thinking helps me prosper in life.

10. To have an UNDERSTANDING, I meditate
so the Divine can talk to me.

11. To have an UNDERSTANDING is to
have a heightened awareness.

Wisdom

WISDOM COMES FROM many sources: books, experts, family, friends, coworkers, neighbors, elders, and even children. Also, we can gain wisdom through lived experience, as well as daily meditative practice. In meditation, information is downloaded from the universal computer. Within this metaphor, we are comparing the universe to a computer as the embodiment of divine intelligence. If we think of it in those terms, then through meditation, wisdom comes to us. Let's deeply process the lived life, be open to the flow of wisdom, and conscientiously do the work of meditation, so that we can become the wise old person.

POWER STATEMENTS

1. WISDOM leads me down the right path.

2. WISDOM protects me as well
    as my loved ones.

3. WISDOM comes through being a
    good student in the school of life.

4. WISDOM turns a student into a teacher.

5. WISDOM is knowledge that has
    been churned and learned.

6. WISDOM is "seeing through" a situation
    so I can learn from the experience.

7. WISDOM is knowing that for
    every sequence of actions, there
    will be a consequence.

8. WISDOM turns the seemingly
    tragic into an opportunity.

9. WISDOM brings security to my life.

10. WISDOM comes through meditative
    practice, so that I am always
    unconsciously conscious.

11. WISDOM is the Higher Self
    talking through me.

Word

THERE IS NOTHING MORE POWERFUL on the planet than the Word, for it is through the Word that we connect with the Divine. The Divine is the creative, organizational, and destructive element within the universe, and as our word connects with the Divine, we must be conscious of what we say. The Word is a creative unit. We must respect the power of the Word.

POWER STATEMENTS

1. My WORD is a creative unit.

2. My WORD can impact myself and others positively or negatively.

3. My WORD uplifts, inspires, and reinforces myself and others to excellence.

4. My WORD must always be diplomatic.

5. My WORD affects my prospective future.

6. My WORD focuses, directs, and manifests consciousness.

7. My WORD is empowered when my subconscious is cleansed.

8. My WORD brings me honor as I consistently honor it.

9. My WORD, when propelled by a passionate heart, has potency.

10. My WORD is potent, whether written or spoken.

11. My WORD is holy, for when I speak, the Divine is speaking.

Acknowledgments

I WOULD LIKE TO ACKNOWLEDGE my manager, Cameron Kadison, who believed in me enough to take me on as a client, which later resulted in the introduction to Nicole Tourtelot, my book agent, for whom I am most grateful. I would also like to express my appreciation to Dr. Karey Pohn, who was there during the initial inception of *The Pocket Guru* and who offered invaluable direction in terms of the structure. And for the many friends who periodically encouraged me to complete the manuscript, such as Damien Smith, Dr. Regina Edmond, and psychotherapist Mike Lane, I honor you. I want to recognize Linda Morris, who assisted in transcribing the drafts. And last but not least, my VP of Operations, TaNisha Cameron, who formatted the edits and helped orchestrate deadlines with the publisher, I thank you. I thank you all!

THE

POCKET

GURU

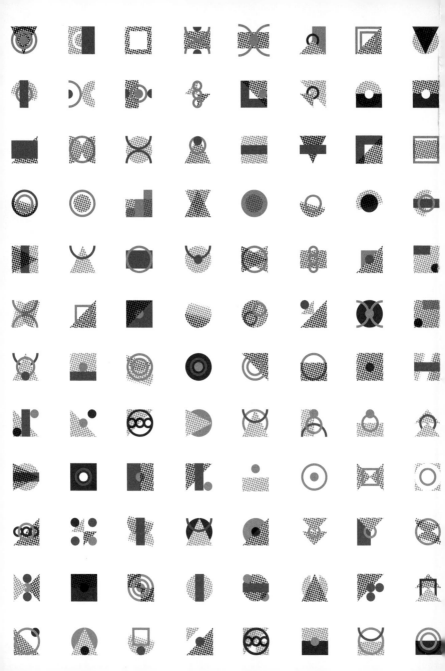